THE BEST
FRONT
RANGE
HIKES

Pikes Peak viewed from Rampart Range to the northeast.

THE COLORADO
MOUNTAIN CLUB
GUIDEBOOK

THE BEST FRONT RANGE HIKES

THE COLORADO MOUNTAIN CLUB FOUNDATION

The Colorado Mountain Club Press
Golden, Colorado

The Best Front Range Hikes

PUBLISHED BY

The Colorado Mountain Club Press
710 Tenth Street, #200, Golden, Colorado 80401
303-996-2743; 1-800-633-4417 | email: cmcpress@cmc.org | www.cmc.org

Founded in 1912, The Colorado Mountain Club is the largest outdoor recreation, education, and conservation organization in the Rocky Mountains. Look for our books at your local bookstore or outdoor retailer or online at www.cmc.org

CONTACTING THE PUBLISHER
We would appreciate it if readers would alert us to any errors or outdated information by contacting us at the address above.

Alan Bernhard	design, composition, and production
Suzanne Najarian	proofreader
Alan Stark	publisher

Cover photo: Mount Neva, seen from the slopes of South Arapaho Peak, by Dave Cooper
www.DaveCooperOutdoors.com

DISTRIBUTED TO THE BOOK TRADE BY
Mountaineers Books
1001 SW Klickitat Way, Suite 201, Seattle, WA 98134, 800-553-4453,
www.mountaineersbooks.org

TOPOGRAPHIC MAPS are copyright 2010 and were created using National Geographic TOPO! Outdoor Recreation Mapping Software. 800-962-1643, www.natgeomaps.com

We gratefully acknowledge the financial support of the people of Colorado through the Scientific and Cultural Facilities District of greater metropolitan Denver for our publishing activities.

NOTE: These hikes were first published in The Best Denver Hikes, The Best Boulder Hikes, The Best Colorado Springs Hikes, and The Best Fort Collins Hikes.

First Edition

Third Printing

ISBN 978-0-9799663-9-2

Printed in Korea

DEDICATION

To the individual members of The Colorado Mountain Club who joined the club for the hiking and climbing and now find themselves deeply involved in conservation issues, educating kids about the outdoors, running the club, and a little book publishing on the side.

They are fulfilling the mission set down by the founders of this club in 1912 when they wrote this mission into the club constitution, a mission that we plan to continue into our second 100 years. "The purposes of the organization shall be to unite the energy, interest, and knowledge of the students and lovers of the mountains of Colorado: to collect and disseminate information regarding the Rocky Mountains on behalf of science, literature, art, and recreation; to stimulate public interest in our mountain areas; to encourage the preservation of forest, flowers, fauna, and natural scenery; and to render readily accessible the alpine attractions of this region."

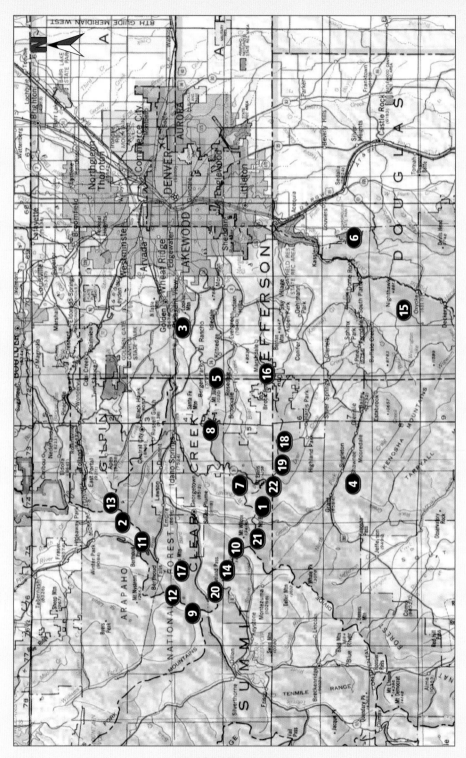

DENVER AND VICINITY

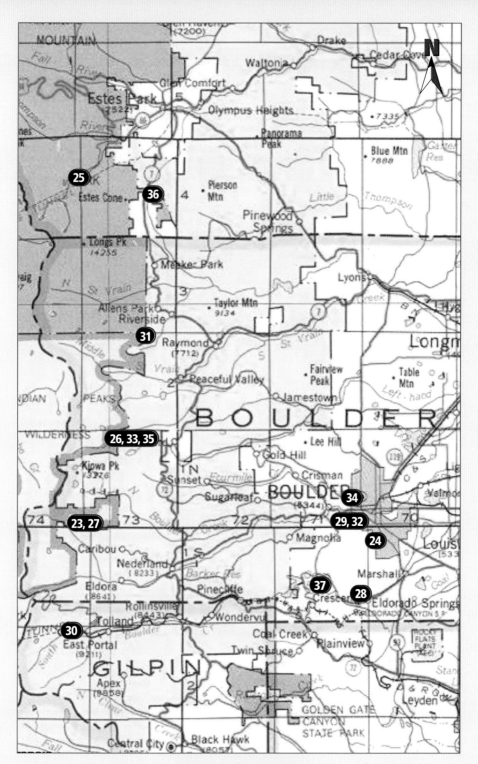

BOULDER AND VICINITY

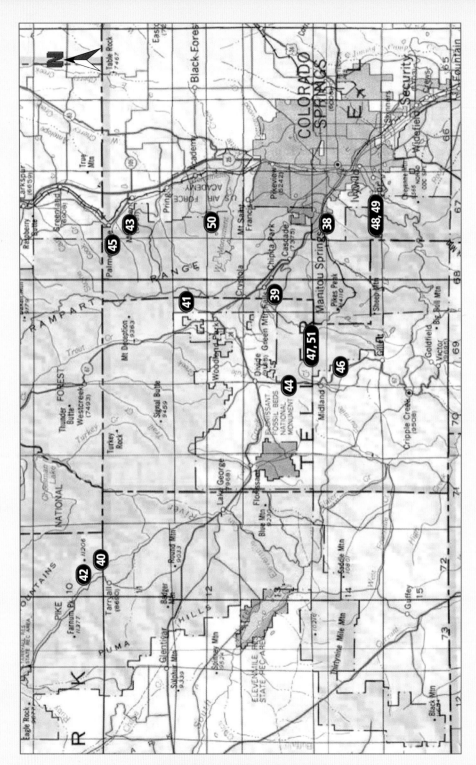

COLORADO SPRINGS AND VICINITY

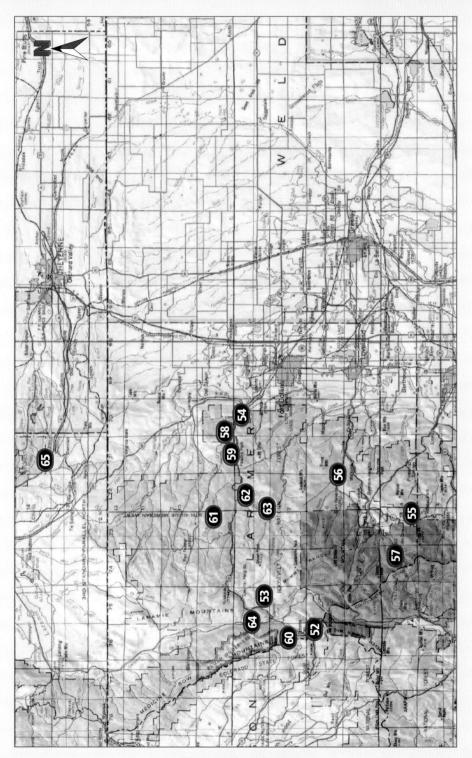

FORT COLLINS AND VICINITY

Contents

Acknowledgments

Greg Long, Jim Groh, John Gascoyne, and Bob Dawson all raised their hands to volunteer as project managers on Group Pack Guides when at CMC group meetings everyone else in the room avoided the gaze of the publisher asking for a volunteer, mumbled something to their neighbors, or turned in their seats to stare off into the distance. For their courage alone, they should be acknowledged, but their contribution went far beyond courage.

These four gentlemen may or may not have known what they were getting into, but in less than a year they organized their committees, steered the committees to agree on the best hikes within an hour's drive of their town, and spent endless hours working with committee members to build a fine series of books that are the antecedent to this book.

Bob Dawson was the project manager for *The Best Denver Hikes*, Jim Groh was the project manager for *The Best Boulder Hikes*, and Greg Long was the project manager for *The Best Colorado Springs Hikes*. A special thanks goes to John Gascoyne, who was not only the project manager for the *The Best Fort Collins Hikes* but has also been the series editor for all of the books.

The following eighty writers and photographers contributed to making this book possible:

Sharon Adams	Eric Erslev
Dan Anderson	Chris Ervin
Kevin Baker	Marilyn Fellows
Lisa Barkley	Susan Friedman
Gail Blanford	Janine Fugere
Steve Bonowski	Tina Gable
Trajn Boughan	John Gascoyne
Bill Brown	Andrew C. Goris
Don Carpenter	Frédérique Grim
Todd Caudle	Joe Grim
Françoise Cooperman	Jim Groh
Pamela Craig	Lincoln Gup
Sandy Curran	Jeremy Hakes
Karen Davis	Nathan Hale
Bob Dawson	Terrie Hardie
Paul Doyle	Ann Hayes
Eileen Edelman	Russ Hayes
Jeff Eisele	Lisa Heckel

Stuart Hiser
Steve Horace
Bob Hostetler
Bill Houghton
Ann Hunt
Linda Jagger
Sandy Jordan
Kristy Judd
John Kirk
Steve Knapp
Jeff Kunkle
Danielle LaRose
Greg Long
Steve Martin
Adam McFarren
Jessica Mehring
Darla Moskowitz
Larry Moskowitz
Carol Nugent
Daryl Ogden
Alex Paul
Matt Pierce

Robert Reimann
James Ribniker
Art Roberts
Janet Robertson
Robert Root
Jilly Salva
Uwe K. Sartori
Erin Sedlacko
Ed Seely
Erin Shaw
Alan Stark
Kate Stewart
Tony Strayer
Dwight Sunwall
Eric Swab
Dean Toda
Jeff Valliere
Don Walker
John Wallack
David Wasson
Paul Weber
Neal Zaun

A bridge crossing Maxwell Creek on the Maxwell Falls hike.   PHOTO BY NATHAN HALE

Introduction

You have picked exactly the right book if you are looking for the best of more than 1,000 possible hiking routes up and down the Front Range. This is the book you want to buy, because *The Best Front Range Hikes* is the work of eighty experienced hikers who picked these sixty-five trails instead of one or two guidebook authors.

In the next several pages we'll describe the Front Range, make some suggestions on how to pick a hike, discuss the basic hiking equipment, including the "Ten Essentials," and conclude with some thoughts on hiking in Colorado.

There are four facts that we'd like you to consider before you use this book. The foothills of the Front Range start at 6,000 feet above sea level, and six points along the Front Range are above 14,000 feet. Before you go for a hike, please think about these four points:

- The weather and trail conditions can change in minutes. Don't get caught without basic gear. See the Ten Essentials later in this introduction.

- If you aren't acclimated to altitude, some fairly strange things can happen to you physiologically. Don't overestimate your abilities.

- While our mountain rescue volunteers, local and state police, and federal rangers are very good at search and rescue, it takes them a while to get to sick or injured hikers, and it is dangerous, expensive work.

- These trails are a trust handed down to us by those who came before. They are a trust to hand down to your children and their children.

GETTING LOCATED

The Front Range is located in central and northern Colorado and is 150 miles long and 40 miles wide. It lies west of the Great Plains and east of the Continental Divide. It includes a number of geographically and geologically distinct subranges, including the Never Summer Mountains and the Mummy Range west of Fort Collins. The Rampart Range and Tarryall Mountains are, respectively, north and northwest of Colorado Springs, and the Pikes Peak Massif is due west of Colorado Springs.

The uplands of the Front Range extend northward into the Laramie Range and northwestward into the Medicine Bow Mountains, both of which lie mainly in Wyoming. On the south, the Front Range is bounded by Cañon

Mount Eva from the flanks of the Mount Bancroft East Ridge.

City and the Arkansas River. The Continental Divide follows the crest of the range southward from the northern end of the Never Summer Mountains to the vicinity of Argentine Pass southeast of Grays Peak and Torreys Peak. Grays and Torreys are the only 14ers that are actually on the Continental Divide. There are four other 14ers in the Front Range—Longs Peak, just south of Rocky Mountain National Park; Mount Evans and Mount Bierstadt, west of Denver; and Pikes Peak, just west of Colorado Springs.

The City and County of Denver is located fifteen miles east of the foothills of the Front Range. It is called the Mile High City because its elevation is exactly 5,280 feet above sea level. The population of Denver is 600,000, and the population of the Denver–Aurora–Boulder area is more than three million. Denver is a transportation hub with a major airport and the intersection of north–south I-25 and east–west I-70. The climate is semi-arid, with rainfall averaging just less than sixteen inches a year. In the summer, the average temperature is in the high eighties during the days and high fifties at night. If you are using Denver as a base for hiking the Front Range, the city is large and traffic can be a hassle. Find lodging on the west side of town or in Golden, which sits right at the base of the foothills. Golden is also the home base of The Colorado Mountain Club.

Fort Collins is sixty-five miles north of Denver on I-25. It sits just east of the foothills and has a population of 140,000. It also has a university and a number of fine microbreweries. Use Fort Collins as a base camp for any number of great hikes up the Cache la Poudre (pronounced pooDER) drainage or in Rocky Mountain National Park.

Boulder, population 95,000, sits right at the mouth of Boulder Canyon and is twenty-five miles northwest of Denver on Colorado 36, which exits from I-25 on the north end of Denver. Boulder is a special place where the person you meet running on a trail can be a Ph.D., a climbing bum, and a great cook—and often all three at the same time. From Boulder, you can base camp for Rocky Mountain National Park and the Indian Peaks Wilderness Area, both within an hour's drive.

Colorado Springs is the second largest town in Colorado with a population of 320,000. The town literally sits under the Pikes Peak Massif just to the west. Located sixty-one miles south of Denver, it is right on I-25. As a base camp, Colorado Springs offers a number of tourist activities as well as some superb hiking just west of town. Try the Barr Trail for something really serious.

PICKING A HIKE

When you get the chance to live, work, and play in a place like the Front Range of Colorado, you simply accept the fact that within two or three miles of your home, you can find a good trail for a walk, and within an hour you can find a great hike in the mountains.   If you are just visiting Colorado and you love to hike trails, well, simply put, this is the place. In the Front Range you can find hikes that are entirely appropriate for kids and seniors; some are even wheelchair accessible. You can also find hikes that will test everything you know about surviving and thriving in the outdoors.

Within an hour of the four major Front Range cites there are more than 1,000 trails maintained by cities, counties, the Bureau of Land Management, the U.S. Forest Service, and the National Park Service. How do you pick?

Most of us ask a friend or an outdoor store clerk. Some of us join clubs like The Colorado Mountain Club and go on club-organized hikes. But most of us go to a bookstore or outdoor retailer who carries guidebooks, thumb through a guidebook, and pick a route. Our selection process is a little haphazard.

If you read and use this book, your selection process for finding a great hike will be enhanced by the experiences of a good number of folks who have picked the best sixty-five hikes between Fort Collins and Colorado Springs. This book is the result of then CMC Executive Director Kristy Judd asking the publisher and the board what The Colorado Mountain Club Press (CMCP) could do to help the groups. The publisher and the members of the CMCP board looked at each other and didn't have an answer to the question,

Mount Sniktau from Watrous Gulch on the Mount Parnasus hike.   PHOTO BY ADAM McFARREN

but within a month we were talking about publishing Pack Guides for all of the CMC groups that wanted to participate. We aren't sure who came up with the idea of the city guides—a number of us have taken credit for the idea—but the fact remains that the four Pack Guides (see the last page) from which this book is compiled were, and continue to be, successes.

The strengths of these Pack Guides are numerous, including full color throughout, clear maps (thanks to TOPO! Outdoor Recreation software), a reasonable price, and a convenient size that fits in a pocket or pack. But the real strength of these Pack Guides and of this book is that a number of outdoor people and CMC members (see the acknowledgments) worked together to decide just exactly what the criteria would be for selecting the best hikes within one hour of their town. They then built matrixes of all of the hikes and began to narrow them down to the best hikes. This book is not the result of one or two authors deciding the best hikes; it results from eighty experienced hikers determining the best hikes.

So how do you pick a hike?

We'd suggest that you read the **COMMENT** sections for the hikes until you find something intriguing. Our eighty writers picked these hikes for reasons that they have explained in the comment sections, which could be summer wildflowers, fall colors, curious geologic formations, a burbling brook, or a view that stretches out to the edge of the horizon.

The **GETTING THERE** sections give clear instructions on how to get to the trailhead. Yup, you'll get lost trying to reach some of these trailheads; we all do. Backtrack to something recognizable or ask a local. Coloradoans tend to be a friendly crowd and can talk endlessly about their trails.

The **ROUTE** section is a description of the trail. One of the many joys of hiking is route finding, so we didn't want to include too much detail but enough information to get you where you want to go. There is one caution: If you get lost above treeline, you can get yourself into some bad spots, get cliffed-out, or actually end up in harm's way. If you sense that you are off-route, backtrack to where you had a sense that you were on-route. Many of these trails are well marked through the trees and have cairns (carefully built piles of stones to mark the way) along the way above treeline. However, cairns can sometimes lead you astray, because they mark an older trail and were not taken down when the trail was rerouted. The trick to navigating with cairns is, when you reach a cairn, take a moment to look downhill to where the last cairn is located and then look uphill to see the location of the next cairn.

BEFORE YOU GO

Experienced Colorado hikers can sound pedantic about the dangers in the mountains and the equipment we carry. Most of us have a story about literally running downhill in front of a threatening thunderstorm only to come across some flatlanders coming uphill wearing nothing but cotton shirts and shorts and carrying a half-empty water bottle that they bought at the local jiffy-mart. To a person, we have always told them that a storm is coming and that they should turn around—and almost to a person, they have ignored the warning and often walked into a very miserable situation.

We carry a good deal of gear in substantial daypacks. If you don't have a daypack, go to a local outdoor store and tell a salesperson what you plan and let him or her fit you for a pack that you can afford, that is well made, that is water resistant, and that will be comfortable with enough adjustments so that it won't bounce around if you have to scramble over some rocks or crawl over a fallen tree across the trail. Depending on the type of gear you carry (more on that in a moment), we think that a pack in the range of 1,500 to 2,000 cubic centimeters is about right.

Boots are also an important consideration. Don't wear brand-new boots

Wildflower garden along the South Boulder Creek Trail on the Heart Lake hike. PHOTO BY TERRIE HARDIE

on a hike. Break them in first. We have tried just about everything from mountaineering boots with a steel shank in them that weighed about ten pounds each to running shoes with aggressive tread patterns. We think that the best bet are high-topped, lightweight trail boots made out of mostly synthetic materials. They are strong and durable and offer decent support and protection.

In the 1930s, The Mountaineers described the Ten Essentials for hikers, backpackers, and climbers. The CMC has adopted those **TEN ESSENTIALS** that, over the years, have been modified.

HYDRATION. You will go through more water than you think you will at altitude. Take two quarts of water with you; for longer hikes, take a water-purification system. If you don't drink until you are thirsty, you have waited too long. Extra water in your car or truck will allow you to hydrate before and after the hike. If you are buying new water bottles made out of poly-carbonate, look for ones that are free of bisphenol A (BPA).

NUTRITION. Eat a good breakfast before you hike. Pack a healthy lunch like a bagel slathered in peanut butter and jelly, an apple or orange, and a chunk of cheese, and carry trail mix and nutrition bars for emergencies.

SUN PROTECTION. Use sunglasses—not the cheapies that you picked up at the gas station but good sunglasses with 100 percent UV protection. Also wear sunscreen with an SPF of 25 or greater, lip balm, and a hat. We like baseball caps (with the bill forward, please) with a cord with two clips in the back to keep it on in the wind. Some prefer boonie hats that are a takeoff on the military models, and some use wide-brimmed hats, but we've found them to be a pain in the wind.

INSULATION. Colorado weather can change in minutes, at any time of the year, so be prepared. Wear wool or synthetic layers of clothing. Yes, polypro can smell a little grody after a day, but, unlike cotton, it will keep you warm when you are wet. Always carry a rain/wind parka and pants and an extra layer of outer clothing. Gloves or mittens, and a wool or polypro watch cap, go in the bottom of your pack. You will be surprised how good they feel to have on in the middle of some wild summer weather.

NAVIGATION. Carry a map of the area in which you are hiking and a reliable—not cheap—compass. We recommend Trails Illustrated maps as being more up-to-date that 7.5-minute quads. It's also a good idea to know how to read a topo map and understand a compass. These are not difficult skills to learn. Be sure to look at your compass occasionally to check your direction instead of pulling it out once you are lost.

ILLUMINATION. Carry a headlamp and extra batteries. We like the kind that has variable intensities and a flasher (for that disco effect). These are handy on predawn starts to 14ers and if you get caught out after dark. Try not to get caught out after dark; it will worry someone who cares about you.

FIRST-AID SUPPLIES. Include a first-aid kit and know how to use it. The kit should include, at a minimum, bandages and gauze, antibiotic salve, blister protection such as moleskin, scissors, disinfectant pads, insect repellent, toilet paper, and a Ziplock bag for used t.p.

FIRE. Carry waterproof matches in a waterproof container that includes a strip of striking material from a paper matchbook or other commercial fire starter and kindling like cotton dryer lint or steel wool. In a pinch, hardened tree sap and dry pine needles will work for kindling. Build fires for survival purposes only; there are already enough fire rings in our mountains, and the fire danger in summer is now always extreme due to all the trees killed by pine beetles.

REPAIR KIT AND TOOLS. A pocketknife or multi-tool, an emergency whistle, a signal mirror, a small roll of duct tape, and eight to ten inches of wire are handy for all sorts of repairs.

EMERGENCY SHELTER. Carry a space blanket and some nylon cord. We like a breathable bivy bag and fleece liner for above treeline. In a pinch, a heavy plastic leaf bag is handy for emergency rain gear, pack cover, or survival shelter. We prefer our bivy bag and hate the thought of some mountain-rescue type finding us huddled in a garbage bag. It's just not a very pleasant image.

This sounds like a lot of gear to haul around on a warm summer hike. Obviously, use common sense, such as leaving the bivy bag home on a three-mile out-and-back hike on a cloudless day. But at one time or another, we have been extraordinarily thankful to have had this gear. Best guess is that with two full water bottles, this should all weigh about twelve to fifteen pounds.

OTHER OPTIONS. Depending on the length of the hike and the season, you may also want to include:

- A foam pad for sitting or sleeping. Some good daypacks come with a foam pad in them.
- A metal cup for melting snow.
- A collapsible snow shovel. A "must have" in avalanche season.
- Walking sticks that are spring loaded and have canted handles. They take some of the weight off of your knees and legs. Practice planting tips quietly to avoid annoying your hiking companions.

This list is intended as a starting place in your preparations for hiking in Colorado; it does not tell you everything that you need to know in the woods and above treeline or how to deal with all emergencies. There are many programs and publications to increase your knowledge base. Please visit The Colorado Mountain Club's Web site at www.cmc.org for more information.

HIKING IN COLORADO

So now you have the right layers of clothing, a good daypack, broken-in boots, and the Ten Essentials. Are you now ready to go hiking in Colorado?

Almost.

Before going, please consider your physical condition and that of your companions, the effects of altitude, the weather, and what you will do in an emergency.

Colorado trails are typically dirt and gravel with water bars to control runoff, and they are often quite rocky, if not all rock. Many of these routes are steep and have a good number of switchbacks. Be careful not to over-estimate your abilities, particularly if you are coming to Colorado to hike from sea level. Give yourself a day or two to acclimate. Going from the flatlands, where the major Colorado cities are located, to 14,000 feet in one day is a gain of 8,500 feet.

As a rule of thumb, if you can comfortably run two miles at home, you should be fine for completing the moderate hikes in this book; if you can run five miles in about sixty minutes or less, the more difficult routes in this book will be little trouble for you.

Ah, but you haven't run anywhere in the last ten years. Fine. Let's say that you want to do a six-mile moderate hike from this book. On a weekend day, measure out three miles from your driveway and walk out and back. How did it feel? Did you do okay? How are your feet? Hiking at 10,000 feet is about a quarter time more demanding on your body than hiking the same distance at sea level or even in the Colorado flatlands of 5,000 feet. Hiking at 14,000 feet is about 50 percent more difficult than hiking in the flatlands.

Assess your physical condition and the condition of your companions. It is no fun being miserable in the mountains. Take it slowly, build up to more difficult hikes, and never be afraid to turn around and try a hike on another day. The mountains will always be there, with the exception of outside of Leadville; come back and try again another day.

Consider also the effects of altitude, where the higher you go, the less oxygen you have available. Altitude sickness can start as low as 6,500 feet, but usually starts in the range of 8,000 to 10,000 feet. The symptoms are nausea or vomiting, fatigue, dizziness, shortness of breath, drowsiness, and periph-eral edema, or the swelling of extremities—the "sausage-finger" effect where your fingers look like little sausages. There are a number of ways to beat it, including acclimating slowly, drinking lots of water, and simply going downhill until you feel better. The odd thing about altitude sickness is that one day you can go to 14,000 feet with few or no symptoms, and on the next hike you can have all sorts of discomfort at 11,000 feet. If you are coming from sea level, ask your doctor about acetazolamide, which seems to help some people make a quick transition to altitude.

The weather in Colorado is spectacular. In the summer it can be seventy degrees at 12,000 feet, and a half hour later it can be forty-five degrees with snow pellets flying straight up in the air and lightning crashing all around you.

There are essentially two ways the weather can kill you quickly in

Looking down the route, Pikes Peak from the Crags hike.

Colorado, and a good number of other spots as well. The first is hypothermia, when wet clothing, wind, and dropping temperatures cause you
to rapidly lose body heat; the second is lightning, which can ruin your day.
All of our comments about types of clothing and layers and rain and wind
protection will keep you out of trouble with hypothermia unless you fall in
a stream or lake.

Lightning is another story. The only protection against lightning is to not
be anywhere close to it. The speed of light is 186,000 miles per second; the
speed of sound is 1,125 feet per second. If you see lightning and count five
seconds before you hear the thunder, the lightning is a mile away. It's a good
rule of thumb that anything less than a thirty-second gap between seeing the
lightning and hearing the thunder is dangerous to your health.

There are two schools of thought. Remember our rule in Colorado about
getting off of summits before noon or earlier if you see thunderstorms
coming your way. The first school of thought is to separate from your
companions so that two people don't get killed by the same lightning strike
and walk downhill about as fast as you can. This isn't the best option,
because lightning tends to flow downhill across the ground in depressions.
Trails are almost always depressions. The second school of thought is to stay
away from depressions, rock overhangs, and large trees below treeline. Put

A beautiful day on the Montgomery Pass hike.

your foam pad and pack on the ground as an insulator. Sit on the pack with your elbows outside your knees and your feet together. Bend over toward your knees, making as small a target as you can. Close your eyes and put your hands over your ears. Think good thoughts. Try to be invisible.

So you understand the concepts of good conditioning, altitude sickness, hypothermia, and lightning, and you have all of the right gear. Yet you or a companion still get injured badly enough that you can't make it back to the trailhead. This is always a tough call. If you stay with the victim, it is going to be a long while before your significant other reports you overdue, and then it will take a long while for search-and-rescue operations to begin and for them to find you. It will be almost impossible for them to find you if you didn't tell someone where you were going and when to expect you back, or if you changed your plans in the field and didn't tell anyone. Get ready for a very long night out. Keep the victim warm and comfortable, build a fire, and remain positive.

Or you can make the victim comfortable and warm, identify precisely where you are on a map, and tell the victim that you are going for help. If you have a cell phone, it sometimes will work at altitude. Call 911 and be very clear about the victim's location. The best bet is to head back to the trailhead. If you run into someone coming up the trail, locate where the victim is on your map, give this person the map, and tell him or her to go for help while you return to the victim. If you don't see anyone, get in your car and drive to the nearest phone and call 911. We can't stress how important it is to know where the victim is located.

Wow. So after all this scary stuff, do you still want to hike the Front Range?

Of course. Thousands of us hike the Front Range from May through October, and we snowshoe or backcountry ski many of the same trails in winter.

The Front Range has a huge variety of amazing trails. Some of them wander through fields of wildflowers or along pristine brooks that cascade downhill toward a line of trees. Some of them go up to mountain lakes where you can doze by the trail in complete peace. And some of the trails take you up to passes and peaks or on traverses that will test every hiking skill you have and show you views for seventy or eighty miles in all directions.

Listen to our thoughts on clothing and equipment, heed our warnings, and enjoy some of the best hiking in the world. And oh, by the way, when you come back, leave no trace of your having been there.

Columbine.   PHOTO BY ERIN SHAW

1. Abyss Lake

BY JEFF VALLIERE

MAPS	Trails Illustrated, Idaho Springs/Georgetown/Loveland Pass, Number 104
ELEVATION GAIN	3,050 feet
RATING	Moderate–difficult
ROUND-TRIP DISTANCE	16 miles
ROUND-TRIP TIME	7–8 hours
NEAREST LANDMARK	Mount Evans

COMMENT: Abyss Lake is an outstanding high alpine lake nestled in a glacial cirque between Denver's nearest 14ers—Mt. Evans and Mt. Bierstadt. Hikers often visit Abyss Lake, situated at an elevation of 12,650 feet, en route to the summits of the surrounding peaks. However, this long dayhike makes an excellent adventure by itself. This hike is technically easy, but its 16-mile length warrants the moderate-difficult rating. Later in this guidebook, look for a difficult-rated hike that includes Mounts Bierstadt and Evans, in a loop route that encircles Abyss Lake—see the Tour d'Abyss description on page 89. Summer and fall are ideal seasons for this hike.

GETTING THERE: From Denver, drive south on U.S. 285 to the small town of Grant. From Grant, travel north on the well-maintained Guanella Pass Road for 5.2 miles to the Abyss Trailhead, at 9,600 feet, on the east side of the road. You can also approach the Abyss Trailhead from Interstate 70, by taking exit 228 in Georgetown and following the road 10 miles over the top of Guanella Pass, then going an additional 7 miles south to the trailhead.

THE ROUTE: The route follows the appropriately named Abyss Lake Trail, all the way to Abyss Lake, closely paralleling Scott Gomer Creek for the first half and then loosely following the Lake Fork for the remaining distance.

The trail starts off at a very casual gradient on an old, closed, four-wheel-drive road and gains very little elevation over the first several miles. The condition of the trail for most of the trip to Abyss Lake is excellent and quite easy to follow. There are numerous creek crossings that have sturdy log bridges across them, although some sections of the trail in the upper basin are quite wet.

After the first creek crossing, at just over 2 miles, the views start to open up and there is an excellent view of Mt. Evans and the 13,780-foot south shoulder

Looking up valley from the lake at 11,730 feet.

of Mt. Bierstadt. The still-wide and well-traveled trail alternates between willows and aspen groves, and passes several beaver ponds along the way.

Approximately 4 miles into the hike, the Abyss Lake Trail intersects with the Rosalie Trail, where they travel the same path for about 0.15 mile. These junctions are well signed and easy to negotiate. The trail soon begins to climb a bit more steeply and follows several well-graded switchbacks up the hillside, where the trees quickly begin to thin and the views of the surrounding peaks improve.

At 11,730 feet, the trail arrives at a small but scenic lake. When this trail description was written, recent beaver activity had flooded the trail to a point where hikers had to either carefully wallow through the very marshy willows on the east side of the lake or take a longer, yet drier, route around the west side.

Above the small lake, the trail becomes a bit rougher, and is wet and muddy for the next 0.5 mile, as it negotiates the last of the willows and blends into a small creek. Once you are out of the willows, it is an easy stroll on the well-worn and easy-to-follow trail across the rolling tundra to Abyss Lake, below the towering walls of the southwest face of Mt. Evans. The lake is located at the very northwest end of the basin that divides Evans and Bierstadt. The trail seems somewhat elusive over the final mile, but you will be rewarded greatly for your efforts. Return by simply retracing your steps.

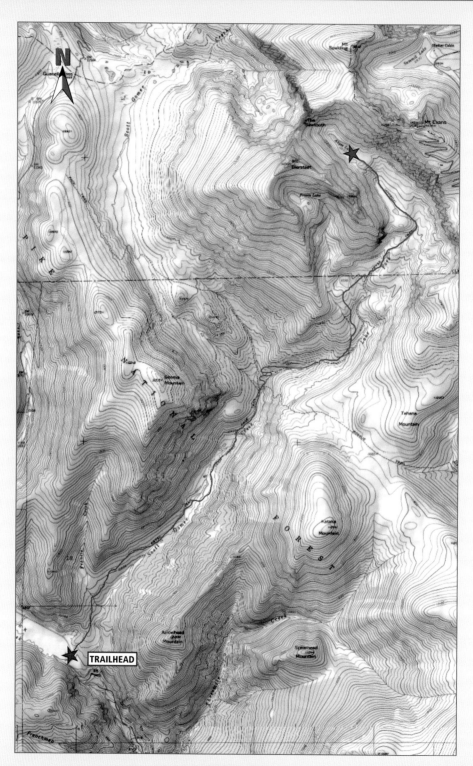

ABYSS LAKE

2. Mount Bancroft (13,250 feet) and Parry Peak (13,391 feet)

BY JOHN WALLACK

MAPS	Trails Illustrated, Winter Park/Central City/Rollins Pass, Number 103
ELEVATION GAIN	2,900 feet
RATING	Moderate
ROUND-TRIP DISTANCE	4.5 miles
ROUND-TRIP TIME	6 hours
NEAREST LANDMARK	Fall River Reservoir

COMMENT: This is the Bancroft Bushwhack! If you don't like a four-wheel-drive road and bushwhacking through some avalanche debris, you won't enjoy this hike. If, however, you like a seldom-traveled route through stunning mountain scenery, this route will reward you with two nice 13ers. A fine ridge walk on the Continental Divide connects Mount Bancroft, 13,250 feet, and Parry Peak, 13,391 feet.

If you've admired the grand peak with three buttresses east of the Mary Jane Ski Area, then you have seen the west face of Parry Peak. The peak is named after Charles Christopher Parry (1823–1890), a botanist and mountaineer on the western surveys, who is credited with, among other things, the discovery of the Engelmann spruce. Parry named the tree in honor of George Engelmann, his botany professor at Columbia University.

GETTING THERE: Just west of Idaho Springs on Interstate 70, take exit 238, the Fall River Road. Zero the odometer at the exit. Follow the Fall River Road to the second switchback, at 6.8 miles. Turn left at the dirt road marked Road 274. This road will require a four-wheel-drive vehicle. The road will get rougher at about 8 miles. The junction to Chinns Lake appears at 9.2 miles. Stay right to go to the trailhead at Fall River Reservoir, at 9.9 miles.

THE ROUTE: The route is a bushwhack north from the Fall River Reservoir to the southeast ridge of Mt. Bancroft. The route follows the broad ridge to Mt. Bancroft, then west along the Continental Divide to Parry Peak. The route finally descends from Parry Peak into the Fall River basin and returns to the Fall River Reservoir.

From the Fall River Reservoir, there is a brown gate with yellow reflectors,

Parry Peak from Bancroft summit.

to the right. Follow the footpath around the gate. About halfway to the top of the earthwork, turn right at the faint double track. Turn left at the grassy knoll and head north along the edge of the trees to an informal campsite by a big rock. There is no trail, so pick your best line up to the ridge, climbing steeply through subalpine fir and bristlecone pine. Bushwhacking skills and trekking poles will be helpful as you ascend the ridge.

Follow the broad ridge west on tundra and over two rock fields to reach the Mt. Bancroft summit. There are great views of Mt. Eva and Chinns Lake to the south and the 4th-class route on the northeast ridge of Bancroft. You could reverse your route from the Bancroft summit, for a shorter day.

To continue on to Parry Peak and complete the Bancroft-Parry Bushwhack, hike west from the Bancroft summit and enjoy the ridge walk, about 0.7 mile along the Continental Divide. From Parry, you can look down onto the Mary Jane Ski Area and anticipate the next ski season.

Descend from Parry Peak, down the rock- and grass-covered slopes to the Fall River basin. Pick your route parallel to the creek. A fisherman's path on the north side of the reservoir will bring you back to the dam.

SIDEBAR: MORE INFORMATION

The 3-mile dirt road between Fall River Road and the Fall River Reservoir passes through private property. Please respect property rights and remain on the road through this portion.

This hike is in the heart of the James Peak Wilderness Area. This is a relatively new (2002) addition to the Colorado wilderness areas.

Further information for this area may be found at: http://www.fs.fed.us/r2/arnf/recreation/wilderness/jamespeak.

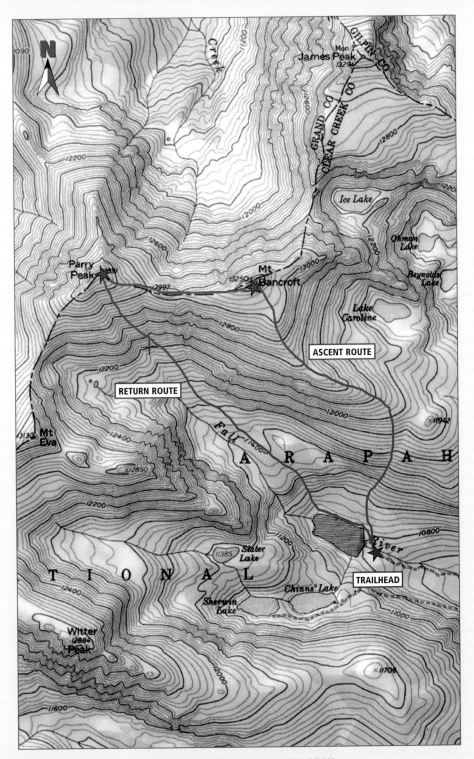

MOUNT BANCROFT AND PARRY PEAK

3. Beaverbrook Trail

BY SANDY CURRAN

MAPS	Trails Illustrated, Boulder/Golden, Number 100
ELEVATION GAIN	1,830 feet total gain and 2,680 feet loss – Chief Hosa to Windy Saddle; Windy Saddle out to the mid/highpoint is 1,300 feet gain and 600 feet loss
RATING	Moderate
ROUND-TRIP DISTANCE	8 miles
ROUND-TRIP TIME	4.5–5 hours
NEAREST LANDMARK	Golden, Buffalo Bill Museum and Grave

COMMENT: Denver Parks' Beaverbrook Trail offers many options and lengths of a hike, but no part of it is really "a walk in the park." The trail often traverses high on the side of steep ravines and there are several rock falls to cross on the east end. That being said, it is a gorgeous hike with a diverse set of views and terrain. You can do the west end down to the ravine (about 2 miles down) and, for variety, head back up on the Chavez Trail— there is a sign indicating the trail as it crosses the creek at the bottom. Or you can start at Windy Saddle and go about 4 miles, with the option of taking the well-marked Gudy Gaskill loop (2.4 miles) to the right. Continue on to a meadow and a flat-topped rock outcrop with great vistas; this is a good place to turn around. Be aware that, on the west end, there are several signs with varying wisdom as to the length of the trail. It would appear the signs along the trail giving mileage to Windy Saddle (8+ miles total) are more accurate than the beginning trail map saying 6 miles end to end, or the sign at the bottom of the ravine giving 6 miles, again, to Windy Saddle!

GETTING THERE: To the Windy Saddle Trailhead, take Sixth Avenue out from Denver to Golden. At 19th Street, turn west up the hill on Lookout Mountain Road and go about 3 miles to a parking lot marked Beaverbrook Trailhead, on the right, at a saddle between the hills. For a car shuttle, leave one vehicle here and continue up Lookout Mountain Road to U.S. 40, alongside Interstate 70. Head west uphill to the Genesee entrance onto Interstate 70. Go 1.0 mile to Chief Hosa, exit 253. Turn back to the right onto Stapleton Drive, a dirt road. Go about 1.0 mile down to the trailhead, where there is a gate. In the winter, the gate is often moved back up the road about 0.5 mile.

The bridge at the bottom of the Braille Walk where the Beaverbrook heads down the ravine.

THE ROUTE: If you want to see it all, I recommend doing a car shuttle starting at the Chief Hosa (west) end and heading to Windy Saddle, the east end. The trail beginning on the west is a lovely Braille Walk (covered wire fence and many signs, all in Braille) for a 1.0-mile circle. At the bottom of the Nature Trail loop, head down the ravine across the wooden bridge; do not head to the right past the outhouse. You will be following red-on-white signs with a "BB" emblem, descending about 1.5 miles to the bottom of the Beaverbrook Creek ravine. Keep an eagle eye out for the trail signs, as there are several false trails at what should be switchbacks, particularly just after a rock face on the uphill side, probably 250 yards past the 7.5-mile marker.

From the ravine and the sign for the Chavez Trail, the trail heads first through some reeds and over rocks, then back up fairly precipitously in places and provides several good views of Clear Creek and the canyon. In about the middle of the 8 miles there is a 2.4-mile additional loop, the Gudy Gaskill Trail, which provides some good overlooks. If you decide to pass up on the Gudy Gaskill Trail, you will instead continue another 4+ miles to Windy Saddle. There are some rock falls to clamber over, around, and through in the last 0.5 mile.

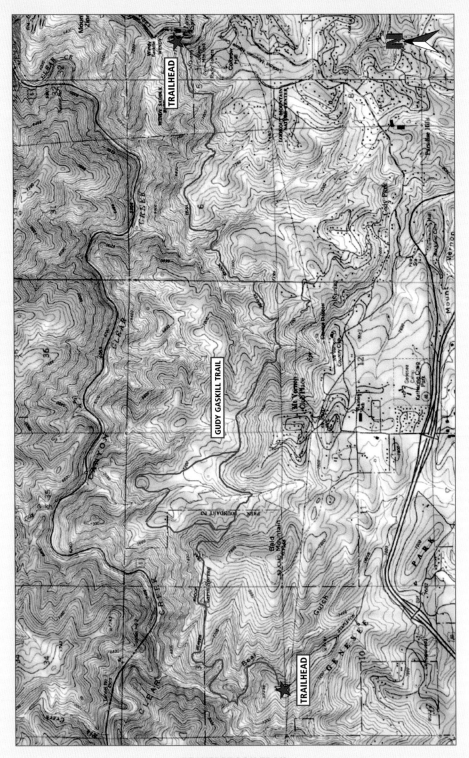

BEAVERBROOK TRAIL

4. Ben Tyler Trail to Kenosha Ridge

BY STEVE KNAPP

MAPS	Trails Illustrated, Tarryall Mountains/Kenosha Pass, Number 105
ELEVATION GAIN	3,400 feet
RATING	Moderate
ROUND-TRIP DISTANCE	11.5 miles
ROUND-TRIP TIME	5–7 hours
NEAREST LANDMARK	Town of Shawnee (along U.S. 285)

COMMENT: The Ben Tyler Trail is an excellent pathway into the beautiful Lost Creek Wilderness southwest of Denver. This trail takes hikers from the easily accessible trailhead along U.S. 285, all the way to treeline. Following Ben Tyler Creek most of the way, hikers enjoy a mix of aspen and pine forests along with mountain wildflowers. The 3,400-foot elevation gain provides a fine workout and great views of the surrounding area. While the trail can be enjoyed year round, late spring and fall are particularly recommended, when the higher mountains are buried in snow. The trail is named after Ben Tyler, who operated a lumber mill and lived in the gulch that bears his name. From the highpoint of this hike, one can access several of the highest peaks in the Lost Creek Wilderness, including Kenosha Peak, Platte Peak, and the Twin Cones. In winter this trail makes a very nice snowshoe outing.

GETTING THERE: From Denver, drive south on U.S. 285. About 7 miles west of Bailey, and 2 miles from the small town of Shawnee, turn left into the small parking area on the south side of the highway. The trailhead offers parking space for only about ten vehicles, but rarely fills up.

THE ROUTE: The route follows the Ben Tyler Trail from U.S. 285 to a wide, flat section at about 11,700 feet on the Kenosha Peak ridgeline. You can continue farther as the trail drops down the Rock Creek drainage to the south, but the ridgeline makes a nice day-hike destination.

There is a wilderness permit station trail register on the trail, just north of the parking lot. Fill out the free permit, deposit a copy in the box, and keep a copy with you. The starting elevation is 8,300 feet. The trail ascends

Heading up Ben Tyler Gulch.

moderately through a series of switchbacks in the first 0.5 mile, and then continues climbing to the southeast as it skirts private property. After about 1.0 mile, the trail enters the Lost Creek Wilderness and stays there for the remainder of the hike. Shortly, Ben Tyler Creek appears on your left. Avoid the first crossing opportunity, as the trail continues on the west side of the creek for about 0.5 mile before eventually crossing it.

After crossing the creek, the well-maintained trail ascends more steeply again, through some nice stands of aspen. This is a spectacular place in the fall. Continue southward as the trail climbs into subalpine meadows and the views open up. In this area, some longer switchbacks begin and it becomes easier to lose the trail when deeper winter snows cover it. At 4.6 miles, and just over 11,000 feet elevation, you will intersect the signed junction with the Craig Park Trail. This trail is a nice alternate route if you want to head to the southeast into Craig Park or climb Platte and Shawnee peaks. For the Ben Tyler Trail, continue to the right.

For the last mile, the trail ascends through the last of the trees and finally breaks out above treeline. There are willows everywhere, and the ground can be soggy in the summer. Views abound, allowing you to enjoy your accomplishment. From the highpoint of the trail, several options exist. Either climb some of the surrounding peaks, descend into the Rock Creek drainage, or call it a day and reverse the trail back to the parking lot.

SIDEBAR: LOST CREEK WILDERNESS AREA

This hike accesses the northern end of the Lost Creek Wilderness Area. Further information for this area may be found at: http://www.fs.fed.us/r2/psicc/recreation/wilderness/lost_creek_wild.shtml.

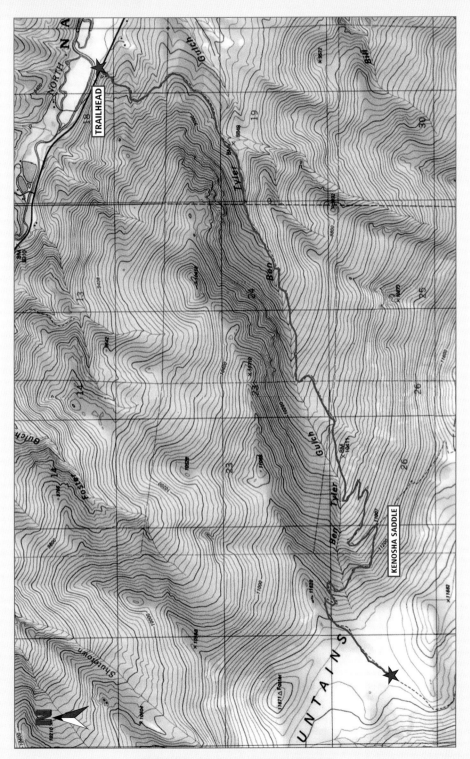

BEN TYLER TRAIL TO KENOSHA RIDGE

5. Bergen Peak (9,708 feet)

BY STEVE BONOWSKI

MAPS	USGS, Evergreen/Squaw Pass, 7.5 minute Jefferson County Open Space, Elk Meadow Park
ELEVATION GAIN	2,000 feet
RATING	Moderate
ROUND-TRIP DISTANCE	9.4 miles
ROUND-TRIP TIME	5 hours
NEAREST LANDMARK	Evergreen Lake, town of Evergreen

COMMENT: One of the outstanding features of this Jefferson County Open Space park is the wide diversity of ecosystems within. The trail is below treeline the entire way, but alternates between forested areas and small meadows that afford views to the northeast and south. The trail to the top of Bergen Peak passes through three different land jurisdictions: Jefferson County Open Space, Colorado Division of Wildlife, and Denver Mountain Parks, with the summit area being part of the Denver Parks system. Three trail junctions along the way from the Stagecoach Boulevard trailhead offer additional shorter or longer hiking options. Hiking this area in the fall affords fantastic views of changing aspen leaves.

GETTING THERE: From Denver, take Interstate 70 to the Evergreen Parkway exit (exit 252) and head south on Colorado 74, past Bergen Park. Continue 2.25 miles to Lewis Ridge Road and turn right, into the parking lot. A second access is available at Highway 74 and Stagecoach Boulevard: turn west on Stagecoach and proceed 1.25 miles to the south parking lot. Open Space maps are available here, and an outhouse is about 100 yards up the trail. The route described below, as well as distance and mileage above, is from the trailhead on Stagecoach Boulevard.

THE ROUTE: The trail goes north for 0.3 mile, to a junction with the Sleepy S Trail, the access route from the east trailhead. Continue to follow the main trail for another 0.7 mile, through ponderosa pine forest with views of Elk Meadow to the north. Turn left at a trail junction onto the Bergen Peak Trail. Follow this trail for 2.7 miles, through the Division of Wildlife property, to an upper trail junction with the Too Long Trail.

The Bergen Peak Trail proceeds through a heavily forested area, but does offer an occasional view of the peak summit area. The trail eventually

View of Mount Evans from near Bergen Peak.

switchbacks up to a ridge crest, with fine views to the south toward Pikes Peak and to the southwest to Mounts Rosalie and Evans. The trail passes through more open ponderosa pine, interspersed with small grassy areas. Once you are on top of the ridge, the trail passes to the northwest, with some up and down hiking to the upper trail junction.

Turn left at the upper junction for an additional 1.0 mile to the summit area. The trail switchbacks up the hillside and then trends west toward an overlook area to the north. The route then passes the west side of the summit area and continues east to its terminus at an open, rocky area with views toward Denver and back again to Mount Evans. A climbers' trail proceeds about 100 yards to the actual summit sign, hidden in the trees. Don't trip over the guy wires anchoring the rescue shack near the top.

Deep forest of the Bergen Peak Trail.

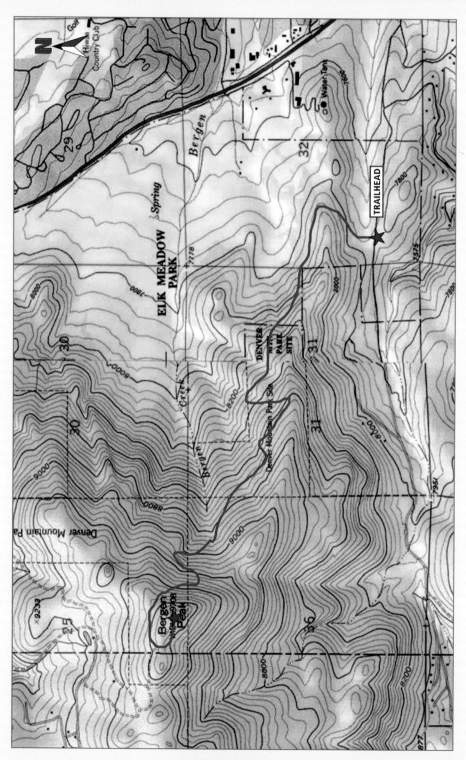

BERGEN PEAK

6. Carpenter Peak

BY SHARON ADAMS

MAPS	Trails Illustrated, Deckers/Rampart Range, Number 135 Free park map at the entrance
ELEVATION GAIN	1,000 feet
RATING	Moderate
ROUND-TRIP DISTANCE	6.4 miles
ROUND-TRIP TIME	3–4 hours
NEAREST LANDMARK	Roxborough Village

COMMENT: Why this hike? Step aside Garden of the Gods ... Roxborough Park has beautiful red rock formations at the beginning of your hike and spectacular views of the Front Range and Denver from the summit. It is open year round, so bring your snowshoes or backcountry skis in the winter. The lush scrub oak and mountain mahogany would provide a beautiful fall hike. If you are looking for a place to take out-of-town guests to experience a taste of Colorado, this is a great choice. It is only a short drive from metro Denver, and the hike stays at a lower altitude.

This is a very family-friendly destination. There are many programs available, through the Visitor Center, for children and adults. Check out the publication "Roxborough Rambles" at the entrance gate for a schedule of activities, or look on their Web site: www.parks.state.co.us/parks/roxborough.

GETTING THERE: From South Sante Fe Avenue: Head south on Sante Fe, U.S. 85, 4 miles south of C470 and exit on Titan Parkway. Head west (right). After 3 miles, the road curves to the south (left) and becomes Rampart Range Road. Continue now south, past Waterton Canyon Road and Roxborough Village. Turn left on Roxborough Park Road and then make an immediate right (in about 50 yards) into the Roxborough State Park Entrance. Stop at the gate and pay the fee or show your Colorado State Parks Pass. Continue on this road another 2 miles to the Visitor Center. It is worth the time to walk through it. Area experts are available to answer questions, and there are books, an auditorium for lectures, interpretive displays, and restrooms.

Driving directions from Wadsworth and C470: Head 5 miles south on Wadsworth from C470 until you come to Waterton Canyon Road. Turn left and head east until the road ends at Rampart Range Road. Turn right and head south on Rampart Range Road. Follow instructions above once you are on Rampart Range Road.

Kids enjoying the summit of Carpenter Peak.

THE ROUTE: The well-marked trail is easy to follow. Begin across a park road from the Visitor Center. The sign reads Willow Creek Loop, South Rim Loop, Carpenter Peak Trail. Follow this trail 0.4 mile to a fork and stay to your right. The next sign reads South Rim Trail, Carpenter Peak Trail. Go another 0.1 mile to another sign and stay to your right. Look for the sign marked Carpenter Peak, Colorado Trail. Cross an open meadow with cottonwood trees and a road. Look for a sign stating Carpenter Peak, 2.6 miles. Now begins the gradual uphill switchbacks. Take special care to watch for wildlife—especially at dawn and dusk. At 1.85 miles from the Visitor Center, you will come to another sign and a fork in the trail. Again, stay right, and follow the signs to Carpenter Peak. The trail then levels out and occasional park benches are available. You will see peaks ahead of you. Carpenter Peak is the one farthest right in the group, with some rocks visible at the top. Continue on, toward the peaks. You will come to the last sign for Carpenter Peak; stay right. There are a few rocks here with a bit of easy scrambling to the top. After basking in the views, retrace your steps back to the Visitor Center.

HOURS:	7:00 a.m. – 9:00 p.m. in the summer
VISITOR CENTER	9:00 a.m. – 4:00 p.m. weekdays,
	9:00 a.m. – 5:00 p.m. weekends summer

Visit their Web site for hours the rest of the year and holiday schedule. No pets, no bikes, day use only.

CARPENTER PEAK

7. Chicago Lakes

BY CHRIS ERVIN

MAPS	Trails Illustrated, Idaho Springs/Georgetown/Loveland Pass, Number 104
ELEVATION GAIN	1,900 feet
RATING	Moderate
ROUND-TRIP DISTANCE	9 miles
ROUND-TRIP TIME	4–6 hours
NEAREST LANDMARK	Echo Lake, Mount Evans

COMMENT: This trail provides access to an incredibly scenic valley, surrounded by rugged cliffs and varied terrain. Due to the high starting point and destination elevation, this hike is seasonal and may not be easily traveled until late spring.

GETTING THERE: Take Interstate 70 west from Denver to exit 240 in Idaho Springs and follow the signs for Mount Evans. Travel south for approximately 13 miles on Colorado 103, to Echo Lake Park. Turn right, onto a dirt road, immediately before the first Echo Lake Park sign, and enter the Echo Lake Picnic Area. Proceed approximately 0.2 mile to the trailhead, at the end of the road. You can also park at the Echo Lake Lodge, located at the intersection of Colorado 103 and Mount Evans Road (Colorado 5). To reach the trailhead from the east, follow Colorado 103 approximately 20 miles, south from the intersection of Evergreen Parkway (Colorado 74) and Colorado 103, near Bergen Park.

THE ROUTE: Proceed to the southwest end of Echo Lake, on the trail that surrounds it. You can pick up the Echo Lake trail from either the Echo Lake Picnic Area trailhead or the Echo Lake Lodge. Your most significant orienteering challenge will be finding the Chicago Lakes Trail sign. From the Echo Lake/Chicago Lake trail junction, proceed southwest on the Chicago Lakes Trail, through the forest surrounding Echo Lake. You will quickly begin to lose elevation as you contour on the cliffs to the south of Echo Lake. Descend the switchbacks into Chicago Creek, on an easy-to-follow trail. After traveling about 1.0 mile, you'll reach your low point of the day, approximately 500 feet of elevation below the trailhead. Cross Chicago Creek on a solid log bridge. Remember that you will have to regain this elevation at the end of the day.

The route through the Chicago Lakes Valley from the Summit Lake Area.

After crossing the bridge, you will come to a dirt road. Turn left on the well-signed route. For the next 1.0 mile, you'll be hiking on the road to the Idaho Springs Reservoir, at 11,600 feet. Continue to follow the road past the reservoir and pass a few buildings on your left. At the end of the road, a sign indicates your entrance into the Mount Evans Wilderness Area. Now, the wilderness experience begins.

Begin to ascend the valley, on a solid trail through alternating patches of dense and burned-out trees. After approximately 1.8 miles from entry into the Wilderness Area, the trail will level out into an open area with amazing views of the surrounding cliffs. You are now approximately 0.7 mile away from the lower of the two Chicago Lakes. As the trail levels out, you will hike through some willows and cross a stream. Lower Chicago Lake, at approximately 11,500 feet, is 3.8 miles from the trailhead. A trail spur allows you to explore the lower lake.

The trail continues to the upper lake, but the route now gets considerably steeper. Hike through, and in some cases over, large boulders as you approach the upper lake, at 11,750 feet. You have hiked 4.5 miles to reach the upper lake. Take a few moments to enjoy views of the surrounding cliffs, the high alpine lakes, the route back down the valley, and, if you're lucky, some bighorn sheep or mountain goats that inhabit the area.

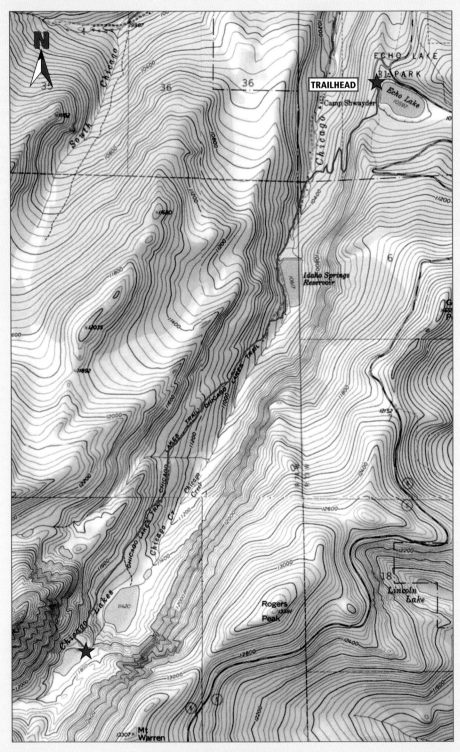

CHICAGO LAKES

8. Chief Mountain (11,709 feet) and Squaw Mountain (11,486 feet)

BY JILLY SALVA

MAPS	Trails Illustrated, Idaho Springs/Georgetown/Loveland Pass, Number 104 USGS, Idaho Springs, 7.5 minute
ELEVATION GAIN	1,800 feet
RATING	Easy–moderate
ROUND-TRIP DISTANCE	4.8 miles
ROUND-TRIP TIME	3 hours
NEAREST LANDMARK	Echo Mountain Park

COMMENT: Are you interested in doing a short and easy hike, but want an actual high-alpine experience? Take your flatlander relatives and friends up these close-in peaks. Popular with families (and dogs), a hike up Chief Mountain offers a place to stroll with small children up to a summit. The last 0.5 mile is above treeline. Despite the steepness, it is well worth the effort. From Chief's rocky summit, hikers are treated to spectacular views of Mt. Evans, the Continental Divide, on over to the Indian Peaks. To complete a fine outing after visiting Chief Mountain, stroll over and visit neighboring Squaw Mountain.

GETTING THERE: From Denver, head west on Interstate 70 and turn off at exit 252, Evergreen Parkway (Colorado 74). Follow the signs to Bergen Park. There will be a light with a sign. Turn right on Colorado 103, continue for 11 miles, and you'll see a sign for Echo Mountain Park on your right. Drive another 1.5 miles and park at the big pullout. This is across the road from the Chief Mountain Trailhead. The trail begins at an obvious post, labeled Chief Mtn Trail No. 58.

THE ROUTE: Chief Mountain is an easy class-2 hike, and is located above the Squaw Pass road. The trail begins up a very short, steep section and then quickly rolls into shady and dense lodgepole pines. Sections of the lower trail are carpeted in aromatic pine needles. This well-marked trail is a great way to share the Front Range foothills with visitors from the lowlands or with beginning hikers.

From the summit of Chief Mountain, you can see Squaw Mountain,

View up the Chief Mountain Trail.

PHOTO BY JILLY SALVA

although from this vantage point it appears unimpressive and cluttered with radio towers. Don't let that discourage you from exploring what it has to offer. Some hikers may opt to follow game trails traversing over to Squaw Mountain. Consider, however, your impact on the land and backtrack down the trail to the junction with old Squaw Road.

Follow the wide dirt road all the way up to the summit of Squaw Mountain. Once on top, you'll discover the historic fire lookout building. There's even a picnic table to have a snack and enjoy the views.

Don't let the easy accessibility of Chief and Squaw mountains lull you into complacency. Storms move quickly in the high country, and lightning is a real threat. If you hear thunder, see dark storm clouds or lightning, head down the trail immediately.

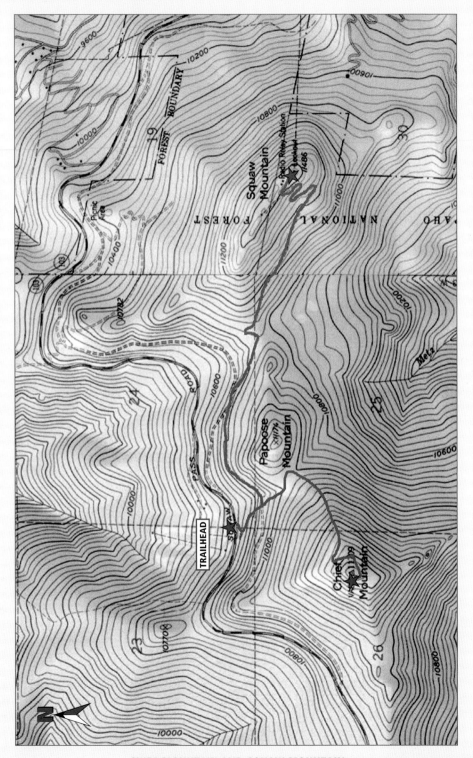

CHIEF MOUNTAIN AND SQUAW MOUNTAIN

9. The Citadel (13,294 feet)

BY ROBERT REIMANN

MAPS	Trails Illustrated, Idaho Springs/Georgetown/Loveland Pass, Number 104
	USGS, Loveland Pass, 7.5 minute
ELEVATION GAIN	2,700 feet
RATING	Difficult
ROUND-TRIP DISTANCE	6 miles
ROUND-TRIP TIME	6–7 hours
NEAREST LANDMARK	Interstate 70, Eisenhower Tunnel

COMMENT: The Citadel is aptly named: From a distance its summit block looks very much like a citadel, with twin towers, or summits, divided by a steep, rocky, but short couloir. The Citadel is not officially named on the USGS topo map, but is on the ridge to the east of Hagar Mountain. The Citadel is a satisfying climb, and it has a variety of terrain and routes. Look for mountain goats on this peak.

GETTING THERE: Drive west on Interstate 70 from Denver to exit 216, the Loveland Pass exit. Turn right onto the gravel frontage road (suitable for passenger cars) and drive eastward for 0.5 mile to the chained iron gate. Park here. This trailhead gives you access to Dry Gulch, the ascent route choice described here. Easy access is also possible via the Herman Lake approach (see page 59).

THE ROUTE: Hike northwesterly on the gravel road on the other side of the gate, a short distance, to a fenced storage area. To the north, you can see the summit. You can also preview your route. Your intermediate objective is a wide grassy ramp, or plateau, about halfway up the slope to the east. From the fenced storage area, proceed north on a faint road. The road turns into a good trail as it soon enters the trees. After crossing the first creek drainage from the east, the trail becomes dubious and meanders uphill on a traverse to the east. Shortly, the "trail" encounters a wide, open grassy slope that contains the second drainage and creek from the east. This grassy slope is your route to the higher grassy ramp, or plateau.

Ascend on the south side of the grassy slope. Follow the grassy ramp north to a high alpine meadow, at about 12,000 feet. From here, you have a choice of routes. You can go to the east, to the saddle at 12,400 feet, or go up the

Views of the surrounding area from high on the Citadel.

slope to the north to get to the ridge. There is a grassy slope about halfway down the ridge. Either way, your next objective is the ridge, proceeding in a southeasterly direction from the summit block. After following the ridge to the base of the summit, you will see why the Citadel is so named.

In snow conditions, you can climb the slope to the east of the ridge, but you need an ice axe, possibly crampons, and the skill to use both. In non-snow conditions, the standard route is to traverse the base of the summit block to the west, to the steep, but short, rocky couloir between the two summits. This couloir faces southwest. An alternative route is to scramble up the first narrow couloir to the west of the approach ridge. This couloir gives you access to the east summit. From the east summit, you hike to the saddle between the east and west summits. There is a drop of about 15 to 20 feet down a chimney to the saddle when proceeding from the east summit. This can be down-climbed. The standard route up the southwest couloir also brings you to this saddle. From the saddle, it is a short climb to the west summit. For the return, retrace your route down Dry Gulch or, as an alternative, head down into Herman Gulch, to the east of the 12,400-foot saddle. Eventually, you will connect with the Herman Lake Trail. This alternative loop route brings you to the Herman Gulch Trailhead that is at exit 218, off of I-70.

SIDEBAR: COULOIR

A couloir is a deep gorge, or gully, formation on the side of a mountain. Refer to the CMC book *Colorado Snow Climbs*, by Dave Cooper, for more descriptions of couloirs in the Colorado mountains.

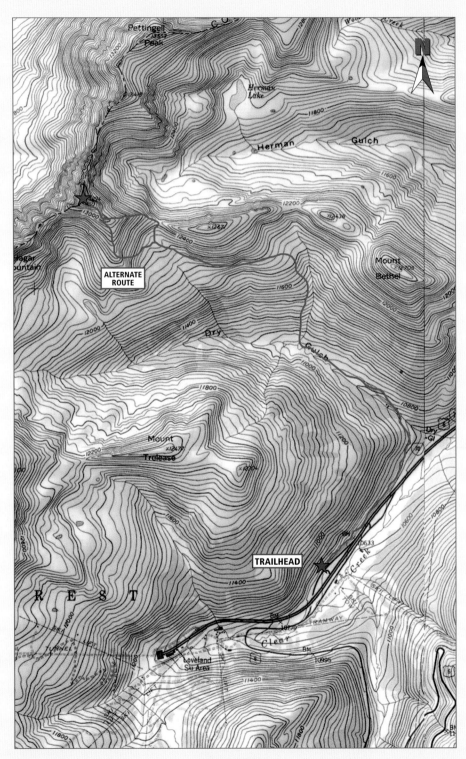

THE CITADEL

10. Mount Edwards (13,850 feet) and McClellan Mountain (13,587 feet)

BY JEFF KUNKLE

MAPS	Trails Illustrated, Idaho Springs/Georgetown/Loveland Pass, Number 104
ELEVATION GAIN	2,440 feet (from the Waldorf Mine)
RATING	Moderate (from the Waldorf Mine) Moderate–difficult (from the Waldorf road)
ROUND TRIP DISTANCE	4.6 miles (from the Waldorf Mine) 16.8 miles (from the Waldorf road)
ROUND TRIP TIME	4 hours (from the Waldorf Mine)
NEAREST LANDMARK	Georgetown

COMMENT: Mount Edwards is a fine alternative to the more popular, and much more crowded, Grays or Torreys Peak climbs, yet offers stunning views of both. Mount Edwards is a "Centennial," or highest-100 peak, ranked the 83rd highest mountain in Colorado. Though mostly off-trail, the climb is not difficult if you start from the Waldorf Mine area. If the road to the mine is too difficult for your vehicle, or closed due to snow, this hike becomes much longer. The east slopes of Edwards and McClellan can provide a feast of wildflower viewing. Late July is a particularly colorful time, though the flowers can hold good color well into August.

GETTING THERE: Take Interstate 70 west from Denver to Georgetown at exit 228. Exit left and pass under the highway, then turn right and go through Georgetown, following the signs toward Guanella Pass. From the start of the Guanella Pass road, go a distance of about 2.6 miles, where a sharp switch-back marks the road to the Waldorf Mine. Park here if you want the full 17-mile hike or, with a four-wheel-drive, continue 6 miles farther to the Waldorf Mine.

THE ROUTE: From the Waldorf Mine, at 11,580 feet, you cannot quite see Mount Edwards, but begin your hike by heading about 0.25 mile south, on the Argentine Pass road, to a creek flowing east from the Mt. Edwards slopes. Leave the road and head west, up the right (north) side of the creek, along a faint climber's trail that switches back and forth up the east slopes of Mount Edwards. If you lose the trail, this is not a problem: simply pick your own

Late July wildflowers on the east slopes of Edwards.   PHOTO BY BOB DAWSON

route and bear slightly north of west toward the obvious saddle between Edwards, on your left, and McClellan, on your right. Once at the 13,420-foot saddle, admire the views down into Stephens Gulch and of Grays and Torreys. Smile at the famous Dead Dog Couloir (on Torreys Peak) from this vantage point, especially if you have been fortunate enough to climb it. The slope down into Stephens Gulch is significantly steeper than what you just came up. From the saddle, head northeast (right) for an easy 0.5 mile to the 13,587-foot summit of McClellan Mountain, your first peak of the day. Retrace your steps to the saddle between Edwards and McClellan and continue southwest for another 0.5 mile, along the ridge to the 13,850-foot summit of Mt. Edwards. Look along the ridge west toward Grays Peak and consider how much fun it would be to continue along the ridge on a future hike.

For now, either head back to the McClellan/Edwards saddle, and retrace your route back to the mine, or, if you want even more ridge-walking fun, consider heading southeast toward Argentine Pass, at 13,207 feet, and going up and over, or around, a couple of 13,000-foot bumps along the ridge. At Argentine Pass, you will be heading in a more southerly direction. Continuing along the ridge and over some more 13,000-foot bumps, the 13,738-foot summit of Argentine Peak is a full 2 miles from Edwards, and it is all above 13,000 feet. If you have the time, the stamina, and stable weather, enjoy your third summit of the day. Horseshoe Basin, to the west, is covered in mines and trails for other peaks in the area, including alternatives on Grays and Torreys. After a rest, retrace your steps north back to Argentine Pass and follow the jeep trail east back to Waldorf Mine.

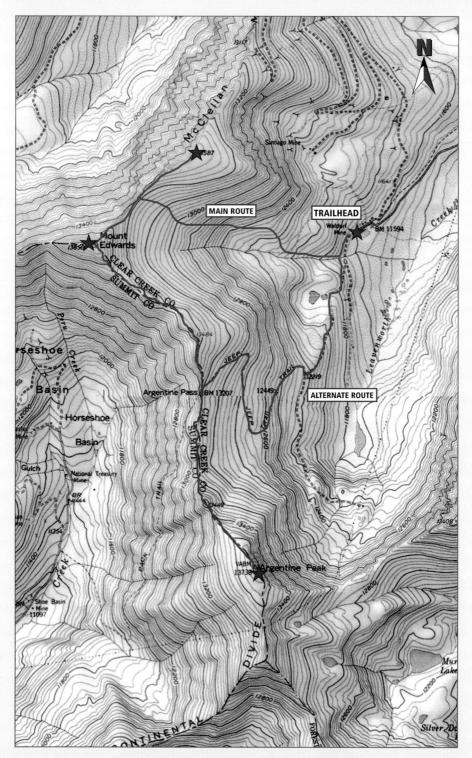

MOUNT EDWARDS AND McCLELLAN MOUNTAIN

11. Mount Flora (13,132 feet), Colorado Mines Peak (12,493 feet), and Mount Eva (13,130 feet)

BY JEFF VALLIERE

MAPS	Trails Illustrated, Winter Park/Central City/Rollins Pass, Number 103
ELEVATION GAIN	3,600 feet
RATING	Moderate
ROUND-TRIP DISTANCE	10 miles
ROUND-TRIP TIME	7–8 hours
NEAREST LANDMARK	Berthoud Pass

COMMENT: Colorado Mines Peak (12,493 feet), Mt. Flora (13,132 feet), and Mt. Eva (13,130 feet) are on the Continental Divide east/northeast of Berthoud Pass. This hike makes an excellent out-and-back, above-treeline excursion any month of the year, as the trailhead is easily accessible year-round. These high ridges along the Continental Divide, often wind scoured, are typically devoid of snow in the winter, allowing easy walking over gentle terrain. However, dangerous avalanche terrain lurks nearby, so route finding, avalanche awareness and preparedness, and sound judgment are essential for this particular hike.

GETTING THERE: From Denver, take Interstate 70 west to exit 232, then U.S. 40 to Berthoud Pass. There is a large parking lot on the east side of the pass. The highway to Berthoud Pass is quite busy during ski season, so plan accordingly.

THE ROUTE: From the southeast corner of the parking lot, at 11,315 feet, follow the dirt road (gated) as it switchbacks its way up the west slopes of Mines Peak, for approximately 1.5 miles and 1,178 vertical feet, to the summit of the peak at 12,493 feet. There are several buildings and large antennas on the summit and, with a little imagination, you can picture yourself atop Mt. Ventoux in France.

Continue northeast along the Continental Divide, descending the gentle, tundra-covered slopes to the Mines/Flora saddle, where you reach a well-worn trail. From here, you will ascend 1,000 feet to the summit of Mt. Flora, as you

Looking back at Colorado Mines Peak from the lower slopes of Mt. Flora.

proceed along the easy ridge for approximately 1.75 miles. The trail to the summit is well travelled and easy to follow.

The 2-mile trip over to Mt. Eva from Flora looks surprisingly distant and involves dropping 650 feet to the 12,475-foot saddle and then regaining the same amount to summit Eva. Although the slopes are somewhat steep dropping to the saddle, and there is no trail to follow, the footing is excellent and the route is intuitive, provided visibility is good. The views are spectacular and the traverse goes by quickly. Remember that on your return trip back to Berthoud Pass you will have to reascend 650 feet to get back to Flora, so make sure you have enough gas in your tank, and the weather is looking good, before committing to Eva.

On the return trip, simply retrace your steps, though it is not necessary to re-climb Colorado Mines Peak. From the Flora/Mines saddle, you can continue on the trail, contouring around the north side of Mines Peak, where it eventually intersects with the dirt road that was used on the ascent.

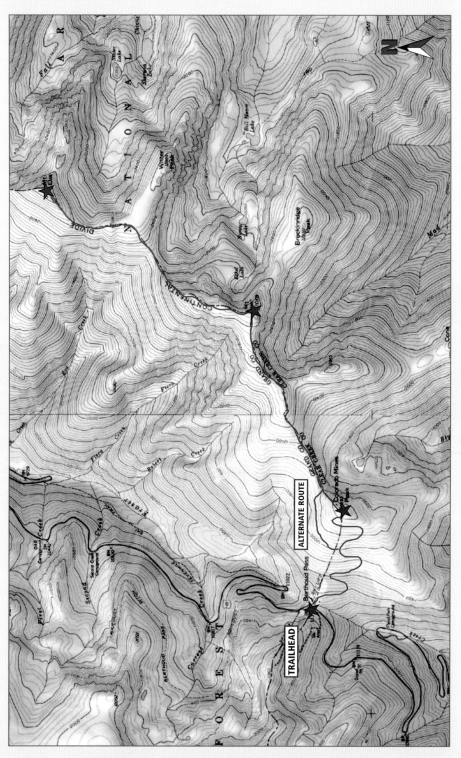

MOUNT FLORA, COLORADO MINES PEAK, AND MOUNT EVA

12. Herman Lake

BY STEVE BONOWSKI

MAPS	Trails Illustrated, Idaho Springs/Georgetown/Loveland Pass, Number 104
ELEVATION GAIN	1,700 feet
RATING	Moderate
ROUND-TRIP DISTANCE	6.5 miles
ROUND-TRIP TIME	4–5 hours
NEAREST LANDMARK	Interstate 70, Eisenhower Tunnel

COMMENT: The trail to Herman Lake offers a pleasant and seldom-steep climb, from just over 10,000 feet, at the trailhead, to a scenic lake, at 12,000 feet. The route is on good trail all the way, although there are some tree root sections to negotiate about halfway to the lake. The area is noteworthy for beautiful wildflower displays in midsummer, with many varieties to be seen. The end of the trail at the lake is below Point 13,294, known informally as the Citadel, and also below Pettingell Peak, at 13,553 feet. A description of climbing the Citadel appears earlier in this guidebook (see page 50). Both of these summits are on the Continental Divide. Although this trail begins at a busy interstate highway, the noise will abate after 15–30 minutes of hiking, and you'll begin to enjoy this beautiful and rather pristine alpine area.

GETTING THERE: The trailhead for both Herman Gulch and Watrous Gulch is located at mile marker and exit 218 on Interstate 70. This is the last exit for westbound travelers before arriving at the Loveland Pass exit and the tunnel. Exit 218 is about 50 miles west of Golden and Lakewood. There is a large parking lot along a frontage road on the north side of the interstate. Note: the east end of the lot is reserved for state-owned vehicles. There is an outhouse at the trailhead and a kiosk with information regarding the Continental Divide Trail.

THE ROUTE: The trail goes north for about 0.25 mile to a T trail junction. Turn left to go to Herman Gulch or right to reach Watrous Gulch. The Herman Gulch trail climbs steeply in the trees on an old road, and eventually goes next to the stream. At this point, you can say goodbye to the traffic noise on the interstate.

The trail trends west and alternates through patches of willows and trees to gain a large meadow area about 1.5 miles from the trailhead. In the summer,

Herman Lake.

PHOTO BY STEVE BONOWSKI

many visitors stop at this meadow to view the flowers. The meadow is also the only place where the author has seen a black bear in the wild in Colorado.

The trail continues west, back into trees, and eventually reaches a second, large, flower-filled meadow where the treeline is visible. Next, the trail turns right and climbs steeply up some switchbacks, goes past the junction with the Continental Divide Trail, and eventually gains a tundra bench. From this point, the trail continues west to the lake, on mostly level surface.

You can ascend Pettingell from the lake by proceeding to its north end and climbing up a steep rock and tundra slope to make a left turn into a shallow gully. This route eventually reaches a scree slope to gain the east ridge of Pettingell. Doing Pettingell adds about another 1,500 feet of elevation gain to your outing.

The Herman Lake Trail is a good snowshoe outing in winter, although the trail can be hard to find in the trees. Skis are generally not recommended, but can work. In early summer, you will encounter residual snow in the trees, making snowshoes essential gear for successful travel at that time.

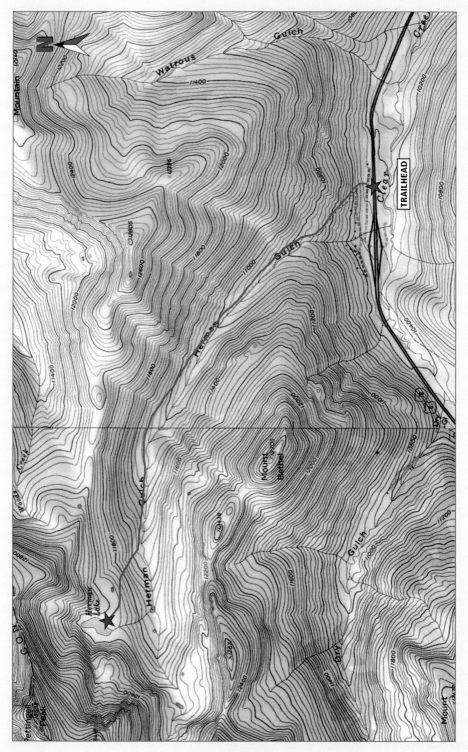

HERMAN LAKE

13. James Peak (13,294 Feet) and Saint Mary's Glacier

BY JILLY SALVA

MAPS	Trails Illustrated, Winter Park/Central City/Rollins Pass, Number 103
ELEVATION GAIN	2,900 feet
RATING	Moderate
ROUND-TRIP DISTANCE	7 miles
ROUND-TRIP TIME	5–6 hours
NEAREST LANDMARK	Fall River Road, Town of Alice

COMMENT: Most Colorado mountaineers and many skiers know Saint Mary's Glacier very well. The site is a true playground for winter sports—even in summer. Although not a true glacier, Saint Mary's is a permanent snowfield and affords year-round access to snow for skiing or practicing mountaineering skills. If you want to wow your out-of-town guests, take them there for a mid-August snowball fight. Less well known, if you travel up the glacier and continue westward, you can climb a fine Colorado 13er. James Peak is a relatively simple climb—by its easiest route—and can even be accessed in winter. Be aware that Saint Mary's Glacier is an extremely popular weekend destination. Once up past the glacier, however, the climb of James Peak should offer you some solitude.

GETTING THERE: From Denver, take Interstate 70 west past Idaho Springs. Turn off at exit 238 and turn right on to Fall River Road. Ascend for 10 miles up past the town of Alice. Look for the Glacier Hike sign on your left; 100 yards past the sign is a public parking lot. The cost for public parking is $5 per vehicle.

THE ROUTE: James Peak is the Gilpin County highpoint and the 5th highest summit in the Indian Peaks Wilderness. The southeast route ascends over Saint Mary's Glacier and can be done year-round. In winter and throughout the spring, knowledge of the snowpack and avalanche hazards will help mitigate potential risks. In the late spring and the summer seasons, hikers should be wary of severe thunderstorms. During this time of year, lightning is a major hazard. Plan your trip so that you are off the summit and down to safety before noon.

Looking back down on St. Mary's Lake.

Begin your hike by following the wide jeep trail for 0.75 mile up to Saint Mary's Lake. Here you'll see the obvious tongue of the glacier stretching before you. Most hikers opt to work their way around the lake to the right of climbers. For those who are more adventurous, you may want to hike up the middle of the glacier to reach Jamaica Flats. Depending on the snow conditions, an ice axe and crampons may be needed for an ascent of the glacier. Staying to the right keeps the angle minimal. In the summer, the snow should be soft enough for an easy ascent with just hiking boots.

Jamaica Flats reveals itself quickly. This area is a flat, mile-wide, open expanse of terrain, peppered with a fanciful array of wildflowers. James Peak rises directly in front of you. Follow the gentle slopes all the way to the summit, either on a winding trail that tends to the left of the slopes, or off-trail on the far right ridgeline. Several rock shelters on the spacious summit mound provide protection from the wind. Spectacular views from the top include Winter Park, the 14ers Grays and Torreys, as well as Mount Evans and the summits of Bancroft and Parry peaks.

Retrace your route for the descent. When approaching Jamaica Flats from this direction, be careful not to get pushed to your right into the wrong drainage. Stay left to reach the top of Saint Mary's Glacier. A favorite activity for most climbers is to glissade or "butt-slide" down the glacier. The resulting wet seat is usually worth the fun involved. Stay to the left, on the gentle slope, while doing this, unless you are an experienced mountaineer and have an ice axe in case your speed increases too much.

JAMES PEAK AND ST. MARY'S GLACIER

14. Torreys Peak (14,267 feet) via the Kelso Ridge

BY BOB DAWSON

MAPS	Trails Illustrated, Idaho Springs/Georgetown/Loveland Pass, Number 104
ELEVATION GAIN	3,100 feet
RATING	Difficult
ROUND-TRIP DISTANCE	7 miles
ROUND-TRIP TIME	6–7 hours
NEAREST LANDMARK	Bakerville Exit on Interstate 70

COMMENT: This route up a very popular Colorado 14er is a classic ridge climb. It affords the aspiring mountaineer an opportunity to experience a taste of 3rd-class climbing terrain, with a bit of exposure in one or two places. You can avoid this exposure by detouring around the more difficult terrain, as described below. Torreys Peak and nearby Grays Peak are very popular summer climbs, but this alternate route will probably not be crowded and offers a fine view of the endless line of hikers heading up nearby Grays Peak. Start very early on this climb to allow maximum chance of success in the safest weather conditions.

GETTING THERE: To reach the Torreys and Grays Peak trailhead, take Interstate 70 Bakerville exit 221 and turn left, crossing over the highway. Continue straight ahead to Forest Service Road 189. This road is rough for passenger cars, but reasonable for four-wheel-drive vehicles. Without a suitable vehicle, you can walk the extra 3 miles to the upper trailhead. Head up this sometimes-steep road, continuing straight at a junction after about 1.0 mile, and drive another 2 miles to the popular Stevens Gulch Trailhead, at 11,250 feet. There are restrooms here and many camping spots.

THE ROUTE: Begin the route by joining the many climbers following the standard route up both Grays and Torreys peaks. From the parking lot, cross the large bridge and follow the obvious trail for about 1.75 miles, to an elevation of 12,300 feet, to where a smaller trail branches off to the right toward an old mine shack.

Just above the mine shack, and to the left, is the low point in the saddle between Torreys Peak and Kelso Mountain to the northeast. The Kelso Ridge

First views of the Kelso Ridge on Torreys Peak. PHOTO BY BOB DAWSON

up to the summit of Torreys Peak is striking. This is an excellent place to stop, eat, and hydrate. Next, head north-northwest up this good side-trail toward the shack, skirting it on the left and climbing to the saddle. Turn left and start up the ridge, now heading just south of west.

Describing in detail the easiest route up the ridge proper is difficult, as there are many variations. The best advice is that if a chosen route becomes too difficult, back off and try something different. The easiest route is typically, though not always, the most beaten-looking path, and swaps between being right on the ridge crest to being just off to either side.

There are two "cruxes" on the route. The first, at approximately 12,700 feet, involves some class-3 scrambling up a roughly 30-foot dihedral, just to the left of the ridge proper. This crux can be bypassed on a climber's trail that heads off to the climber's right, around the ridge, and involves some steep scree climbing. Though the bypass is technically easier, staying on the main route up the dihedral is overall a better route.

The second crux occurs at around 14,000 feet, not far below the summit. This is the infamous "knife-edge" ridge of Torreys, and involves some very exposed scrambling across a pointed ridge. Your author has more than once scooted across this section on his buttocks, legs carefully straddling the ridge.

As with the first crux, this short section can also be bypassed with a faint climber's trail that descends off to the right and traverses around the knife-edge, then reascends to catch the main climber's trail past the knife-edge. If any of your party are averse to exposure, this might be a better alternative.

Once past the knife-edge, it is easier going the last couple of hundred feet to the summit of Torreys Peak. Descend by heading down the "normal" Torreys Peak route toward nearby Grays Peak. Once at the Torreys/Grays saddle, follow the obvious and nicely marked trail until it intersects with the Grays Trail and finish your descent.

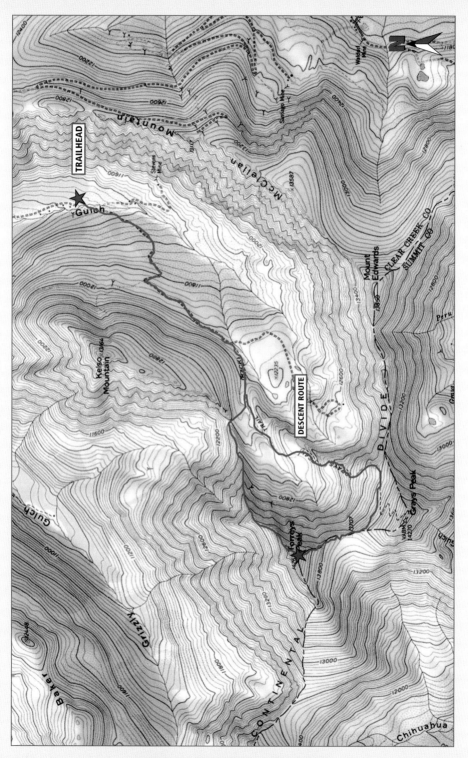

TORREYS PEAK VIA THE KELSO RIDGE

15. Long Scraggy Peak (8,812 feet)

BY DWIGHT SUNWALL

MAPS	Trails Illustrated, Deckers/Rampart Range, Number 135
ELEVATION GAIN	2,000 feet
RATING	Moderate–difficult
ROUND-TRIP DISTANCE	11 miles
ROUND-TRIP TIME	6+ hours
NEAREST LANDMARK	Town of Buffalo Creek

COMMENT: Long Scraggy Peak stands prominently along the South Platte River, southeast of the town of Buffalo Creek. Excellent views of beautiful granite towers protruding from the forest can be seen in all directions. Lost Creek Wilderness, Mt. Evans Wilderness, and the Rampart Range surround this isolated summit. Long Scraggy Peak makes a fine winter hike when the higher peaks are deep in snow. It is also a fine summer hike through the shady Pike National Forest. While formerly known routes accessed this peak north of the Long Scraggy Ranch, this area is now badly scarred from the Hayman fire and the access road is closed. The route described here uses a closed forest service road, but the entire approach is in an unburned area south of the ranch that then uses the old trail up the northwest slopes to the summit.

There are shorter, more direct, ways to the summit than this route, but this is a good choice. The only private property concern is the Long Scraggy Ranch; its boundaries are plainly visible on the Trails Illustrated map. Alternatively, you can call the ranch and ask for permission to start hiking from their property. This would shorten the route by several miles.

GETTING THERE: From Denver, drive southwest on U.S. 285 (Hampden Avenue). Turn left at Pine Junction on County Road 126 (Pine Valley). Drive 13 miles, passing Pine and Buffalo Creek. Drive south on 126 another 4.5 miles and park at the entrance to Forest Service Road 530, or at the Little Scraggy Trailhead parking area.

THE ROUTE: Hike Forest Service Road 530 east and then north. This road is closed to unauthorized motorized travel, but it is a good dirt road. A mountain bike works very well for this section of the hike. At mile 4.5, you will be about 1.0 mile north of the peak. Begin to look to your right for an unused jeep road, at the north end of the hill you are currently on. The jeep road is just before Road 530 turns left and descends. The road looks

Long Scraggy Peak.

completely unused and is partially covered with dead tree branches and new tree growth. You will be following the 7,600-foot contour line on your map as it leaves the road and heads for a meadow, about 200 paces northeast. It is shown as a white spot on the map.

An unnamed, intermittent creek flows through the meadow. A faint trail follows the creek going southeast, uphill toward Long Scraggy Peak. A few hundred yards up the stream, you should start seeing sections of the trail on the north side; the farther upstream you go, the more visible the trail becomes, and you will start seeing cairns. Watch closely, as the trail is easy to lose, but it does have many small cairns. Ascend for about 0.75 mile until you arrive on the ridge, about 500 feet north of the peak. From here, you can either follow the trail on the west side or, as some prefer, simply take the ridge all the way to the summit. The top is easily attained on solid rock, with a few class-3 moves. Enjoy the expansive views, including massive Pikes Peak to the south.

SIDEBAR: CLASS THREE

"Class-3 moves" means that you need to employ your hands, as well as your feet, in order to safely and effectively complete a particular movement.

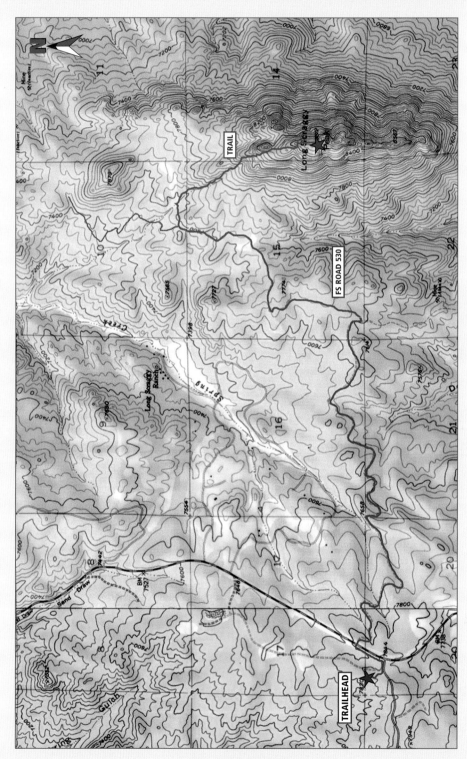

LONG SCRAGGY PEAK

16. Maxwell Falls

BY NATHAN HALE

MAPS	Trails Illustrated, Boulder/Golden, Number 100
ELEVATION GAIN	800 feet
RATING	Easy–moderate
ROUND-TRIP DISTANCE	2.4 miles, including the Cliff Loop
ROUND-TRIP TIME	2–4 hours
NEAREST LANDMARK	Evergreen

COMMENT: This short-but-sweet hike begins with a gentle trail through montane forest with lush vegetation where it parallels the creek. Next, hike through dense lodgepole pines until the trail drifts onto the surrounding mountainsides and ridges.

Maxwell Falls can be reached from two different trailheads. The trip from the upper trailhead to the falls is a short 15–20 minute hike, with little elevation change. Starting from the lower trailhead gives you a longer, more strenuous outing. Either hike can be combined with the Cliff Loop, a scenic loop that adds to the difficulty and provides views from a loftier perspective.

The falls themselves are rather difficult to access, and most people settle for the view at the overlook along the main trail. If you choose to approach the base of the falls, the easiest access is by a number of small social trails that leave the main trail below the falls and follow the creek. Be careful, as many of these trails are intermittent and can involve tricky and precarious rock scrambling.

GETTING THERE: Reset your odometer at the stoplight in downtown Evergreen and follow Jefferson County 73 for 1.0 mile, then turn right onto Brook Forest Road. The lower trailhead is at 4.4 miles, but can be difficult to distinguish among the many driveways along this road. For the upper trailhead, pass the Brook Forest Inn at 5.7 miles and continue as the road becomes Black Mountain Road, just past the old livery stable. Reach the upper trailhead at 7.2 miles.

THE ROUTE: The trail is obvious as it leaves the lower trailhead and ascends on a wide, generally smooth path into the national forest, following the drainage of a small, unnamed stream. The trail crosses the stream and comes back to climb over a broad ridge, to switch to the Maxwell Creek drainage. At the top of this ridge, the trail passes through a small clearing and descends

View of Maxwell Falls from the overlook.

through a lodgepole forest down to Maxwell Creek, then crosses on a sturdy bridge and again begins a gentle ascent.

The lower Cliff Loop junction is just past the creek crossing. The signage is straightforward when coming from the lower trailhead; it can be a bit confusing when approached from the upper.

The trail is nearly flat as it closely follows Maxwell Creek. This gentle section ends abruptly as the trail switches back steeply up the hillside. It is below these switchbacks that the social trails used to access the falls leave the main trail. Again, be careful on these trails and try to leave minimal impact.

A rocky overlook onto the falls sits at the top of the switchbacks; it offers great views down the valley as well. The upper Cliff Loop junction is 5–10 minutes beyond the falls. Another 10 minutes' hiking brings you to the upper trailhead.

The Cliff Loop is a side trail that climbs up the west side of the Maxwell Creek drainage and follows the cliffs overlooking Maxwell Creek. This trail leaves the main trail halfway between the falls and the upper trailhead and loops around to meet the main trail, just west of the creek crossing. The climb from the lower junction is relatively steep, but levels out after reaching the cliffs. The steep ascent is harder than the steady climb of the main trail, so it is slightly easier to start from the upper junction and descend this section. The trail is wide and easy to follow and, while it follows near the cliffs, generally keeps its distance. For the best views, you'll want to leave the trail briefly to skirt the edges of the cliffs.

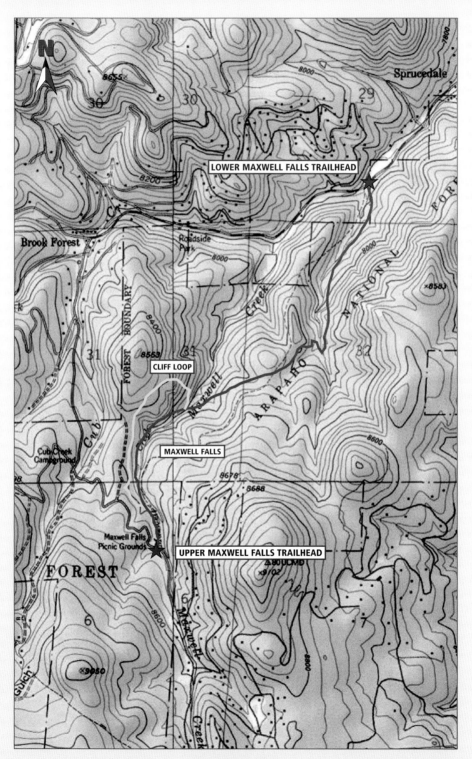

MAXWELL FALLS

17. Mount Parnassus (13,574 feet) and Woods Mountain (12,940 feet)

BY ROBERT K. REIMANN

MAPS	Trails Illustrated, Idaho Springs/Georgetown/Loveland Pass, Number 104
ELEVATION GAIN	3,700 feet (for both mountains)
RATING	Moderate
ROUND-TRIP DISTANCE	7 miles
ROUND-TRIP TIME	7–8 hours
NEAREST LANDMARK	Interstate 70, Eisenhower Tunnel

COMMENT: Mount Parnassus undoubtedly takes its name from Mount Parnassus in southern Greece, located near the Delphic Oracle. In Greece, Mount Parnassus is a home of the Muses and a center of artistic and poetic activity. Colorado's Mount Parnassus was a favorite climb for the well-remembered Colorado Mountain Club member Eckart Roder, who would climb it each fall around the time of his birthday. Watrous Gulch, Mount Parnassus, and the Woods Mountain area are CMC favorites. Watrous Gulch is a beautiful valley with scenic views of Torreys Peak and other nearby mountains. The area offers a variety of moderate and pleasant climbs and routes, partially on- and partially off-trail. Parnassus and Woods are also excellent winter climbs, due to the low avalanche risk, good workout, and high elevation attained.

GETTING THERE: Take Interstate 70 west of Denver to exit 218, one exit past the Bakerville exit, and the second exit prior to reaching the Eisenhower Tunnel. Turn north into the trailhead parking lot. There is a restroom at the trailhead. This is the Herman Gulch Trailhead, but it is also used to access Watrous Gulch, one drainage to the east.

THE ROUTE: After hiking about 0.25 mile, the trial forks. To the left is access to Herman Gulch; access to Watrous Gulch, our goal on this hike, is to the right. At 25 feet after turning right, the trail turns to the left. Follow this gradually inclining trail through the aspen and pine-forested area for about 0.75 mile to Watrous Gulch, where the trail flattens out. Head up the valley on the trail on the west side of the creek. After about 0.3 mile, the trail crosses the creek. A sign indicates a trail intersection with the Bard Trail. In

Views of nearby Torreys Peak.

PHOTO BY ADAM MCFARREN

non-snow conditions, the good Bard Trail can be taken to the south; it traverses the west slope of Parnassus. When the trail crosses the south ridge of Parnassus, it is time to hike north up the ridge to the summit of Parnassus, at 13,574 feet. There are several false summits on the way to the true summit. A worthwhile side trip, from the summit east across a ridge, leads to Bard Mountain. For the return trip, proceed north and down the rolling slope to the saddle between Parnassus and Woods, at 12,500 feet. From the saddle, you can proceed north up the gentle slope to Woods Mountain, at 12,940 feet, and eventually proceed west back down to Watrous Gulch, for a circle loop. Upon reaching the wooded area down the slope from the saddle, a short and simple bushwhack of a couple hundred yards will take you to a creek that intersects the trail up Watrous Gulch. Proceed south down the Watrous Gulch Trail until it intersects with the Bard Trail.

For winter hikes, the usual route proceeds in a northerly direction up Watrous Gulch from the intersection with the Bard Creek Trail, about 1.0 mile, to a creek drainage coming from the saddle between Parnassus and Woods, at about 11,400 feet. At this point, there is some bushwhacking required for a couple of hundred yards, in a northeast direction through a stand of trees. There is often a snow-packed trail through the woods. An alternative route proceeds north up the Gulch and circles to the east. Once through the trees, or after circling the Gulch, proceed to the saddle between Parnassus to the south and Woods to the north. Retrace your steps for the return route.

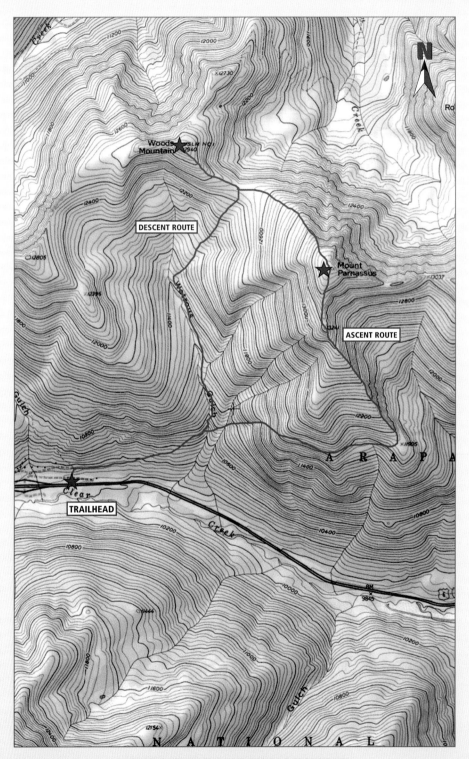

MOUNT PARNASSUS AND WOODS MOUNTAIN

18. Pegmatite Points (12,227 feet)

BY SHARON ADAMS

MAPS	Trails Illustrated, Deckers/Rampart Range, Number 135
ELEVATION GAIN	2,900 feet
RATING	Moderate
ROUND-TRIP DISTANCE	7.5 miles
ROUND-TRIP TIME	5–6 hours
NEAREST LANDMARK	Fall River Reservoir

COMMENT: The Pegmatite Points are really an extension of Rosalie Peak's east ridge; see Rosalie Peak at page 80. There are numerous rock-scrambling opportunities that don't exist on nearby Rosalie's gentle summit mound. This great year-round trail is particularly nice in the fall, as the colors are brilliant and plentiful. It is also excellent for a winter snowshoe hike, although the road may not be open beyond the Deer Creek Campground—adding an additional 1.6 miles round-trip. Take the time to explore the rocks: pegmatite veins can contain feldspar crystals, creating an overall pink appearance. This is a popular hike, so arrive early as the parking lot fills up on weekends.

GETTING THERE: Take U.S. 285 southwest from Denver, past the town of Conifer, then another 7 miles to the town of Pine Junction. Go another 4.4 miles and make a right on County Road 43A, at a traffic light. Follow west and it very shortly intersects with County Road 43. The signs will now read CR 43, or Deer Creek Road. Drive 8.1 miles to Deer Creek Campground. At mile 6.9, the road comes to a V. Stay to the left on CR 43. This road is paved until the last 0.8 mile, and then changes to a good dirt road. Continue past the campground 0.8 mile to the Deer Creek Trailhead.

THE ROUTE: The trail is well marked and fairly easy to follow. From the parking lot, you will soon come to a National Forest Service sign-in station. Fill out a Wilderness Use Permit and attach one part to your backpack. There is no fee involved. A junction in the trail is just past the sign-in. Stay to your right on the Tanglewood Trail. This trail follows the Tanglewood Creek for the first part of the hike. This part of the trail is lush with trees and bushes. You will cross the creek three times, over good bridges, and eventually over a couple of log bridges. After the third good bridge, you will come to a second trail junction. The Rosalie Trail is left, but stay right, on the Tanglewood Trail. This junction is at about 9,980 feet.

Easy scrambling on one of the Pegmatite Points.

Continue on and up on the easy grade. At around 10,900 feet, you will cross the creek for the last time and head into a more forested area of evergreens. Follow some switchbacks until you get to treeline at about 11,500 feet. The trail opens into a wide and open willow meadow with spectacular bristlecone pine trees scattered around. Take the time to use your camera for these beauties.

The trail leads you to the right of the willows. You can see the saddle between Mt. Rosalie and the Pegmatite Points. Once on the saddle, follow the ridge to the right, toward the rock formations. These mark the beginning of the Pegmatite Points. The first big rock outcropping is not the highest—it is just the beginning of the fun. Keep going back farther over the rocks, to find the highest point, at 12,227 feet. Allow plenty of time for some fun and easy class-3 scrambling in this rock playground and enjoy some beautiful views of Mt. Evans.

There are no ranked summits on Pegmatite Points, but if you wish to add one, you can return to the saddle and climb Mt. Rosalie, at 13,575 feet.

Return back to your car by retracing your steps from the saddle.

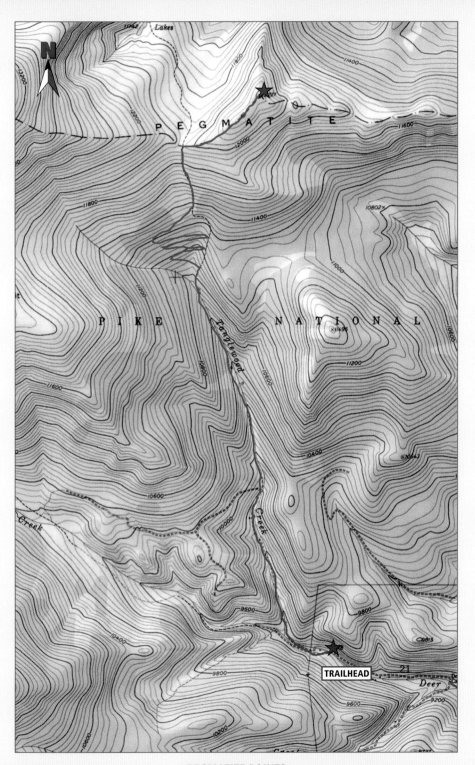

PEGMATITE POINTS

19. Rosalie Peak (13,575 feet)

BY JOHN WALLACK

MAPS	Trails Illustrated, Idaho Springs/Georgetown/Loveland Pass, Number 104
ELEVATION GAIN	4,300 feet
RATING	Moderate
ROUND-TRIP DISTANCE	11 miles
ROUND-TRIP TIME	8–9 hours
NEAREST LANDMARK	Mount Evans

COMMENT: Rosalie Peak, at 13,575 feet, packs a punch. While the 4,300-foot elevation gain is a good conditioner hike, the unique views of Mount Evans and Mount Bierstadt make the hike worthwhile. The upper part of the route goes through a bristlecone pine grove. This is an excellent tundra hike with ptarmigan, marmots, and wildflowers along the way. Albert Bierstadt, the famous 19th-century landscape painter, named the current Mount Evans after his wife, Rosalie. In 1870, Mount Evans was renamed after John Evans, the second governor of the Colorado Territory. The name Rosalie was then given to this 13,575-foot peak.

GETTING THERE: From Denver, drive south on U.S. 285. About 4 miles after Pine Junction, turn right onto Park County Road 43A, at a traffic light and gas station. Zero your odometer. At 6.9 miles, the road splits, with Deer Creek Campground (CR43) to the left and Meridian Campground (CR47) to the right. Stay left. At mile 8.1, there is a turn for the Deer Creek Campground. The road to the trailhead is to the right, with trailhead parking at mile 8.9.

THE ROUTE: The route follows the Tanglewood Trail to the saddle, at about 12,000 feet, near Pegmatite Points. From the saddle, the route follows the broad ridge due west, to the summit of Rosalie.

The starting elevation is 9,280 feet. Within the first five minutes, there is an unmarked trail to the left (the old Rosalie Trail). Stay right. The first mile includes three wooden footbridges over the stream. At about 1.0 mile, or 9,800 feet, the trail junction of the Rosalie Trail (TR603) is to the left and Tanglewood Trail (TR636), to the right. Stay right on the Tanglewood Trail. After about an hour of hiking, you'll reach a fine clearing. The gentle summit of Royal Mountain, at 11,495 feet, is to the east. Keep hiking, you have only 90 percent still to go.

The summit of Rosalie Peak.

PHOTO BY JOHN WALLACK

The trail is mostly well defined. At about 10,600 feet, a willow-filled clearing affords the first clear views of Pegmatite Points and the ridge to Rosalie. About 10 minutes after that clearing, there is a potential place to get off-route: two beaten paths in a lodgepole area. Stay to the right; you'll hear the Tanglewood Creek and soon encounter a log stream crossing.

The trail makes some wide switchbacks as the gradient increases just below treeline. Many maps still reflect the old, more direct, route. The trail soon leaves the trees and angles up through a grove of bristlecone pine. Ten more steep minutes and you'll be at the saddle.

The views south from the saddle are worth taking a break to enjoy. To the southwest, the first rounded peak south of Rosalie is Bandit Peak. Beyond Bandit, Logan marks the north side of U.S. 285. The Kenosha and Tarryall ranges stretch to the south. Pikes Peak can be seen on the distant horizon.

The summit appears close but, alas, it is a false summit. There is still about a 1,600-foot elevation gain from the saddle. The hike up to Rosalie from here follows the broad ridge for 1.3 miles. On a good day, this is a delightful tundra stroll, rich in tiny wildflowers. There is a pilot rock that makes a good target on the false summit. From the sea of weathered rocks, proceed up the final few hundred yards to the summit cairn. At 13,575 feet, the views of Mount Bierstadt and Mount Evans are impressive. Return as you came.

SIDEBAR: MOUNT EVANS WILDERNESS AREA
This hike accesses the southern end of the Mount Evans Wilderness Area. Further information for this area may be found at: http://www.fs.fed.us/r2/arnf/recreation/wilderness/mountevans.

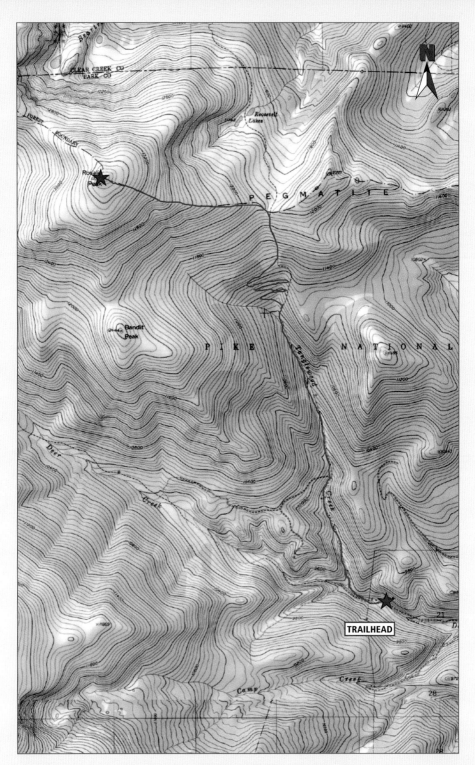

TRAILHEAD

ROSALIE PEAK

20. Mount Sniktau (13,234 feet) and Grizzly Peak (13,427 feet)

BY CHRIS ERVIN

MAPS	Trails Illustrated, Idaho Springs/Georgetown/Loveland Pass, Number 104
ELEVATION GAIN	3,800 feet
RATING	Difficult
ROUND-TRIP DISTANCE	7.5 miles
ROUND-TRIP TIME	5–6 hours
NEAREST LANDMARK	Loveland Pass

COMMENT: This climb of two fine Front Range 13ers is an enjoyable but physically serious hike: there is a good deal of elevation gain and much of it is on the return trip. The entire hike is above treeline, at an elevation above 12,000 feet. In summer, keep constant watch for potential thunderstorms— there is no easy way to make a fast retreat if a storm approaches. In winter, great care must be taken to avoid dangerous cornices that form along the ridge. By remaining on the ridgetop proper, however, this can provide an excellent winter outing.

GETTING THERE: The trailhead is located at 11,990 feet, on the summit of Loveland Pass. Take exit 216, off Interstate 70, just east of the Eisenhower Tunnel and follow U.S. 6 west for about 4.5 miles. The parking area is well signed.

THE ROUTE: From the parking area, start by climbing east up a set of rock stairs. A wide, easily identifiable trail leads east-northeast toward your journey along the Continental Divide. The trail continues until the well-rounded summit of Point 12,915. From this point, look southeast, where you can see the challenge ahead for your trip to Grizzly Peak, as well as excellent views of Torreys Peak and Grays Peak. But first, turn to the northeast and follow the trail toward your initial destination, Mount Sniktau.

As you approach Point 13,152, the trail traverses slightly to the west (left) of the talus sitting between you and the highpoint of Point 13,152. Follow a broken trail through the rocks to the top of Point 13,152, where Mount Sniktau will finally come into view. Stay on the trail as it descends along the ridge and then ascends to the summit of Mount Sniktau. Enjoy the

Mount Sniktau from Point 13,152.

panoramic view of several Colorado mountain ranges. You have traveled about 1.8 miles from the trailhead.

After reviewing the long ridge route to Grizzly Peak from Mount Sniktau, retrace your steps along the ridge back to Point 12,915. This is a good time to evaluate the weather and determine if an attempt on Grizzly Peak is prudent. You are now closer to your car than you are to Grizzly's summit.

To continue on to Grizzly Peak, begin to hike southeast until you locate a well-defined trail that follows the ridgeline toward Grizzly Peak. As you descend to the saddle, look for cairns that indicate a connector trail to the west (right). This can provide an alternative to reclimbing Point 12,915 on your return to the trailhead. Continue along the trail toward Point 13,117 (Cupid) as the trail becomes less defined, but is well cairned. The route skirts to the right of the Cupid highpoint, where the remainder of the route comes into view.

As you've learned by now, the route continues with ups and downs as you pass additional bumps along the way. The trail skirts to the left of some rocks as you continue toward Grizzly Peak. At last, you approach the climb, up a well-worn trail toward Grizzly Peak's summit, at 13,427 feet. After enjoying the views of the Continental Divide and surrounding mountains, prepare for the return trip to Loveland Pass. This is dominated by numerous ascents and descents back along the long ridge. As mentioned, you can avoid reclimbing Point 12,915 by looking for a trail junction marked by cairns as you approach Point 12,915. In winter conditions, or anytime there is potentially unstable snow, avoid dropping below the ridgelines and attempting this or any other shortcut.

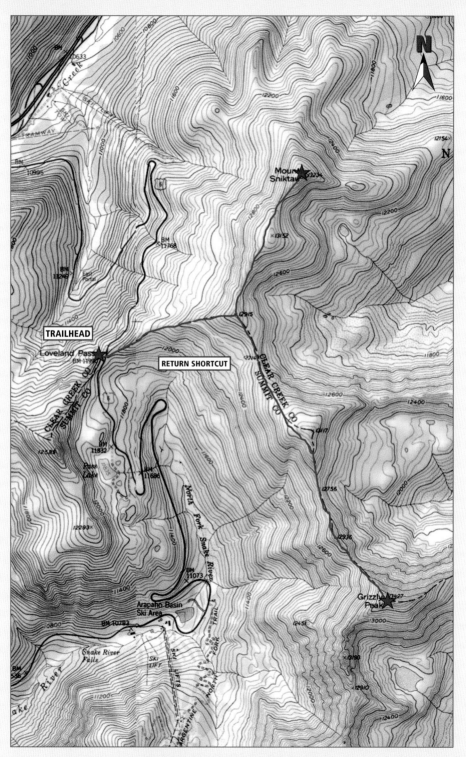

MOUNT SNIKTAU AND GRIZZLY PEAK

21. Square Top Mountain (13,794 feet)

BY SHARON ADAMS

MAPS	Trails Illustrated, Idaho Springs/Georgetown/Loveland Pass, Number 104
ELEVATION GAIN	2,100 feet
RATING	Moderate–difficult
ROUND-TRIP DISTANCE	7 miles
ROUND TRIP TIME	5–6 hours
NEAREST LANDMARK	Guanella Pass

COMMENT: Why climb Square Top Mountain? Square Top is Colorado's 111th highest peak and makes a nice loop hike. It affords great views of the Sawtooth Ridge between Bierstadt and Evans to the east, and the Colorado high country to the west. Beautiful alpine lakes grace this fine hike on the west side of Guanella Pass. Look east to see dozens of people climbing nearby Mount Bierstadt, a popular 14er, while enjoying your solitude on this wonderful 13er. Square Top Mountain can be climbed all year and skied in the winter. In winter, call the Clear Creek Ranger District, 303-567-3000, for Guanella Pass road closures.

GETTING THERE: Guanella Pass can be accessed either from Interstate 70 or from U.S. 285. For the first option, take I-70 west from Denver to Georgetown at exit 228. After exiting left and passing under the highway, turn right and go through Georgetown, following the signs toward Guanella Pass. There has been construction on this road, but it shouldn't be a problem. From U.S. 285, turn right at the town of Grant and travel north for about 13 miles. There are many campsites along Guanella Pass road if you want to make your adventure an overnighter. Call Clear Creek Ranger Station or South Platte Ranger Station for information.

THE ROUTE: From the parking lot at the top of Guanella Pass, the initial trail is an informational hike with signs along the way. After approximately 100 yards, turn right at a fork and leave this signed path. You will descend a little bit and head across a meadow full of willows. Pass a trail-closed sign on your right. To the right, you will see the northeast ridge. Continue a little farther along the path and turn off the trail to the right, heading toward this ridge. Once on the ridge, at approximately 12,400 feet, simply follow it up toward the peak. There is a short scramble over a rocky area that opens up to

Square Top Lakes grace the descent.

a wide saddle. From here, you can see Square Top Lakes (upper and lower) to your left and Silver Dollar Lake to the right. Cross the saddle at 12,800 feet and continue up the ridge, staying more toward the left, as there is generally more loose rock on the right. As you approach a large rock formation with a small notch in the middle, bear to the left for the easiest route up. As the trail levels out, it is approximately 0.25 mile past false summits to the true summit.

True to its name, Square Top is a plateau top, nearly 0.5 mile long. Walk to the west end to gaze deep into the heart of Colorado's high country.

To complete this loop, begin by retracing your steps along the top plateau and turn off to your right before you reach the last rock scramble that you came up. Next, head down and to your right, across open area. Avoid the cliff area by continuing more toward your right. Again, you will see the lakes below as you follow the southeast ridge down. Once off the ridge, curve slightly to the left, aiming toward the upper lake. Walk past the upper and lower lakes and eventually join the well-marked trail by the lower lake, and then back toward the parking lot. The trail through the willows can be marshy with a few small water crossings.

Of note: Be on the lookout for the Mt. Evans mountain goat herd that very often wanders through the area.

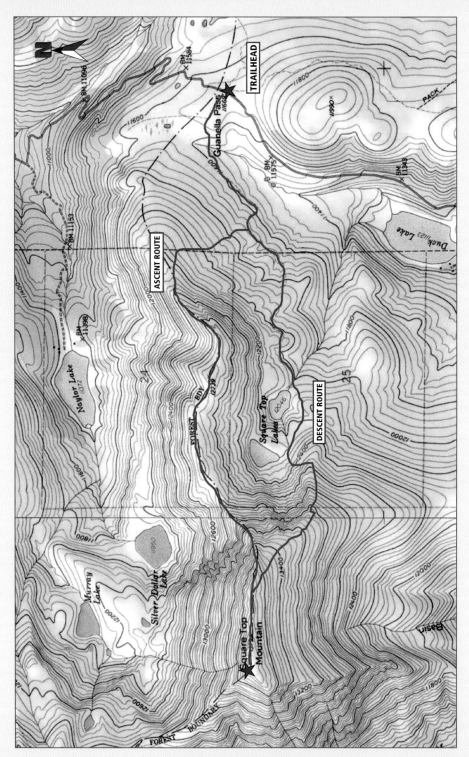

SQUARE TOP MOUNTAIN

22. The Tour d'Abyss:
Mount Bierstadt (14,065 feet) and
Mount Evans (14,270 feet)

BY BOB DAWSON

MAPS	Trails Illustrated, Idaho Springs/Georgetown/Loveland Pass, Number 104
ELEVATION GAIN	3,000 feet
RATING	Difficult
ROUND-TRIP DISTANCE	6 miles; add 4.5 miles if road is closed above Summit Lake
ROUND-TRIP TIME	7–8 hours
NEAREST LANDMARK	Echo Lake & Mount Evans Road

COMMENT: This is a beautiful and exciting loop route, and the most difficult hike in this book. The loop completes a high circuit around Abyss Lake, hence the unofficial name. This route is not for beginners, but for more seasoned rock scramblers. Good route finding is required to keep this loop below the technical 5th-class level. If you have the experience and confidence, this is a marvelously satisfying route. The author has climbed this eight times in as many years. The loop affords the shortest route that starts at a road and includes the summits of the two Front Range monarchs, Mount Evans and Mount Bierstadt.

GETTING THERE: This trailhead is only reasonably accessible in the summer, when the Mount Evans road is open at least up to Summit Lake. From Denver, take Interstate 70 west to Idaho Springs and take exit 240. There is a sign for Mount Evans before this exit. Head south and follow Colorado 103 approximately 13 miles to Echo Lake. An alternate approach is to take Colorado 103 west from Bergen Park for 18 miles to Echo Lake.

From the east end of the Echo Lake Lodge, turn on to Colorado 5, the Mount Evans road. Pay your fee at the station and head generally south up the road, following the many switchbacks, for 9 miles to Summit Lake. Before Memorial Day, or after Labor Day, the road past Summit Lake may be closed, depending on snow conditions. Continue up the road from Summit Lake for an additional 2.3 miles, past two small switchbacks. On a large switchback, at 13,300 feet, there is a small parking area, large enough for a half dozen cars. This is the trailhead.

Some of the four-legged mountaineers that frequent the area. PHOTO BY BOB DAWSON

THE ROUTE: This unique way of climbing a 14er actually starts as a *descent*. Head south from the parking area, for less than 0.2 mile, to the low point of the saddle between Evans and Epaulet. Look closely for a decent climbers' trail that descends west down a steep scree gully to the beautiful Abyss Lake valley below. Head due west, navigating around the southern end of a small lake, at 12,360 feet, then climb a steep but otherwise easy grassy slope, catching the east ridge of Mount Bierstadt at approximately 13,100 feet. Choose a line and climb up and over Point 13,420; a reasonable 3rd-class route exists just left of the ridge proper. Once past Point 13,420, the crux of this part is to navigate around Point 13,641. The easiest likely route is to head somewhat down and right of the ridge, finding grass ledges on the northeast slopes of the ridge. These ledges tend to be slightly easier the farther one descends. Once a good ledge system is found, contour along them beyond Point 13,461, until an easy route is found back up to the ridge. Once back on the ridge, follow it on the path of least resistance, all the way to the summit of Bierstadt.

After your summit visit, head down slightly east of north toward the infamous Sawtooth formation, between Bierstadt and the long west ridge of Mount Evans. The goal now is the low point of the saddle, between Bierstadt and the Sawtooth, at approximately 13,300 feet. There is a decent climbers' trail that descends along the east side of the ridge.

Just past the low point are a gendarme and the crux of this part of the route. Study it carefully and pick a line up and over it, tending to climbers' right for the easiest route. There are numerous cairned 3rd-class options.

Once over this difficulty, climb back to the ridge proper, approaching the point where the route crosses over from the east to the west side of the ridge. Look for cairns and follow the climbers' trail over to the west side. From here on the route is easier, though quite exposed. Follow along the ledges on the west side on an obvious path. Climb along this loose dirt and rock ledge system, bearing left then up a steeper section, finally passing through a notch and abruptly off of the west face of the Sawtooth. Once out on easy ground, hike east toward the long west ridge of Evans, eventually hooking up with a well-cairned trail on the south slopes of this ridge. This final ridge run is only 1.0 mile long, but may seem longer.

Enjoy the summit of Mount Evans as long as you can stand the loud and perfumed tourists fresh from their drives up the road, then head down the road back to your car, at the switchback at 13,300 feet. For a more direct descent, there is a decent climbers' trail that crosses directly over the road switchbacks.

SIDEBAR: MORE BETA

The Tour d'Abyss circles Abyss Lake; Climber Chris Wetherill coined the name. A "gendarme" is an isolated, spiked pinnacle perched atop a mountain ridge.

The infamous Sawtooth Ridge reflected in Abyss Lake.   PHOTO BY JEFF VALLIERE

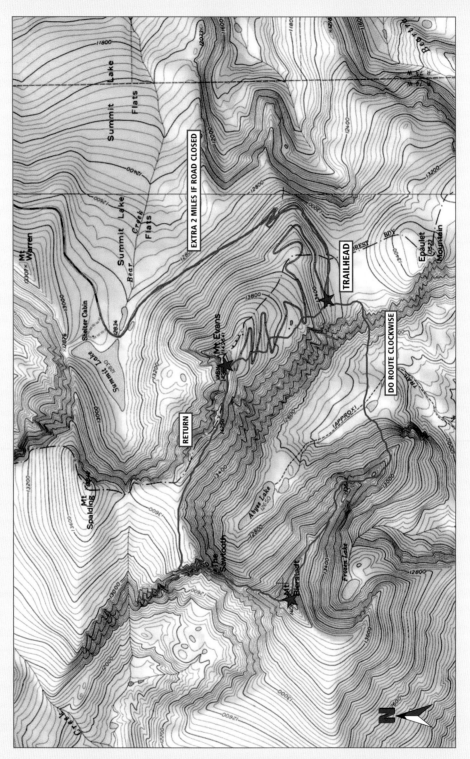

THE TOUR D'ABYSS: MOUNT BIERSTADT AND MOUNT EVANS

23. Arapaho Pass and Caribou Pass

BY LINCOLN GUP

MAPS	Trails Illustrated, Indian Peaks/Gold Hill, Number 102 USGS, East Portal and Monarch Lake, 7.5 minute
ELEVATION GAIN	2,369 feet
RATING	Moderate
ROUND-TRIP DISTANCE	8.6 miles
ROUND-TRIP TIME	5–6 hours
NEAREST LANDMARK	Nederland

COMMENT: Explore a rainbow of wildflowers along a track from a glacial valley to over 12,000 feet on the Continental Divide. From late spring through midsummer, you'll travel across steep, flower-studded meadows penetrated by sparkling cascades. And along the highpoint of your climb, views of vivid lakes nestled beneath acute summits accompany you to a secluded high pass where white-tailed ptarmigan frequent the rock-studded carpet of tiny, ground-hugging flowers and plants.

GETTING THERE: From Boulder, drive west on Canyon Boulevard (Colorado 119) for 15 miles to Nederland. At the roundabout in Nederland, steer left (south) onto South Bridge Street (Colorado 119 and 72) and continue 0.6 mile to Eldora Road (County Road 130). Turn right toward the Eldora Ski Area, stay right when the road forks to the ski area, and continue through the Eldora townsite. The pavement ends after the town and it becomes Hessie Road. At the Hessie turnoff, at 0.8 mile, turn right onto Fourth of July Road. Follow this for a rocky, potholed, and gullied 4 miles to the trailhead. The road beyond Eldora is generally impassable from winter though midspring.

THE ROUTE: Ascend the stairs on the north side of the uppermost parking lot to start the Arapaho Pass Trail. After you pass into the shade of pine and fir trees and turn west, look alongside the dozens of trailside seeps and rivulets for the yellow petals of heartleaf arnica and the tiny inverted magenta petals of shooting stars.

Numerous avalanche paths intersect the subalpine trail, creating lush meadows alight with a spectrum of blooms, including geraniums, harebells,

Arapaho Pass and Lake Dorothy from the summit of South Arapaho Peak. PHOTO BY LINCOLN GUP

gentians, rosy paintbrush, and bluemist penstemons. At 1.0 mile up the trail, cross the first of several cascades on rocks that can be icy in early morning. Lavender and white columbines, the Colorado state flower, prosper in this terrain. Don't let the rushing waters distract you from the herds of the aptly named elephant's head flowers, with their tiny pink trunks and sizeable ears.

At the Diamond Lake Trail sign, at 1.1 miles, continue uphill to the right. As you approach the top of a steeply sloping meadow, at 1.5 miles, look to your left for a small rocky overlook. Pause here to soak in the alpine panorama before continuing up.

After a brief rise, the trail crosses krummholz and willow flats, below the craggy face of South Arapaho Peak. Ponder the lifestyle of an early 20th-century gold miner as you pass the Fourth of July Mine to the right (north) of the trail at the 2.0-mile mark. An old drum winch and steam boiler adorn the yellow tailings pile surrounding the remains of a 2,000-foot-deep shaft. Leave treeline and follow the rough remains of an old road 1.2 miles up to the Arapaho Pass sign at 11,900 feet, a minute's walk east of the Continental Divide.

Proceed straight ahead on the Caribou Trail toward Caribou Pass for 0.3 mile to drink in views of beautiful Lake Dorothy, the crowning jewel in the Mount Neva cirque tiara. Just a few minutes off the trail, Lake Dorothy's craggy shoreline provides picturesque views of Neva's steep, striated walls and the Arapaho peaks to the northeast.

Ascend west 0.1 mile to the highpoint of the journey, at 12,100 feet. From here, observe the trail ahead and contemplate your options. The route to Caribou Pass is the remains of an unfinished, narrow road blasted across the cliff face. In places, it's no wider than two shoes and abuts a precipitous 800-foot drop to Caribou Lake. The path to the pass may be blocked by steep snow until late summer.

If you elect to proceed, traverse past rock bands of dark gneisses and schists for 0.7 mile to the solitude of Caribou Pass. Multihued stones, short grasses, purple primrose, and tiny forests of pink moss campion dominate the tundra landscape. In this harsh, windswept environment, plants that are only inches tall may be decades old. If you have the time, a 0.5-mile side trip to Satanta Peak will be rewarded by edge-of-the-world views of the line of peaks arching along the Continental Divide. Return by reversing your course.

SIDEBAR: STAYING IN TOUCH

Many mountain areas lack cell phone reception. It is common for hiking parties to get separated at times into smaller groups, as hikers tend to travel at their own pace. If this is a possibility for your group, you can stay in touch with portable walkie-talkie radios, which typically have a range of up to 5 miles. Be sure to charge your radios in advance, configure them to the same channels, and have them turned on whenever your group becomes separated on the trail. It is the official stance of The Colorado Mountain Club, however, as well as common sense, that the safer policy is never to split up your group.

Alpine sandwort and spring beauty along the Arapaho Pass Trail.   PHOTO BY LINCOLN GUP

ARAPAHO PASS AND CARIBOU PASS

24. Bear Peak Loop via Fern Canyon and West Ridge

BY LINCOLN GUP

MAPS	USGS, Eldorado Springs, 7.5 minute CMC Trail Map, Boulder Mountain Parks and Nearby Open Space Boulder Open Space and Mountain Parks Trails Map
ELEVATION GAIN	2,905 feet
RATING	Difficult
ROUND-TRIP DISTANCE	8.0 miles
ROUND-TRIP TIME	4–5 hours
NEAREST LANDMARK	NCAR

COMMENT: This track offers a steep, forested climb bounded by sandstone monoliths to a prominent, rocky summit. From the top, you'll take in the round-the-compass views extending from Longs Peak, located to the north in Rocky Mountain National Park, and all the way down the spine of the Continental Divide to some 14,000-foot peaks, south of I-70. The descent passes rolling meadows before nestling alongside a stream in a deep canyon for the trip back to the bottom of Bear Peak.

GETTING THERE: From the intersection of U.S. 36 and Table Mesa Drive on the south side of Boulder, proceed west on Table Mesa Drive. Continue past Broadway Street. Table Mesa winds its way up through a neighborhood, eventually depositing you in the parking lot at the National Center for Atmospheric Research (NCAR) Mesa Laboratory. Park in the large semicircular parking lot.

THE ROUTE: Walk west along the parking lot road to find the Walter Orr Roberts Trail, on the north side of NCAR. Follow the trail west across the mesa, staying left where possible. Before the end of the mesa, the trail takes a dive to the left and down at 0.2 mile, then jogs back west. Follow the trail another 0.5 mile, down through a meadow, over the Dakota Hogback ridge, past a green water tank, and then down to the Mesa Trail. Go left (south) on the Mesa Trail and then right (west) at the junction with the broad Bear Canyon Trail, until it crosses Bear Creek. Things look up from here, as this is the lowest point of the trip; you are about to gain 2,400 feet in 1.8 miles.

Bear Peak at sunrise.

PHOTO BY LINCOLN GUP

Continue 0.5 mile south, and up, on the Mesa Trail until you can turn right onto the Fern Canyon Trail.

As you move steeply upward, you'll be guided between the towering walls of the Fountain Formation sandstones.

At 2.3 miles, pause for the view from the saddle, at 7,400 feet, nestled between Bear Peak and a smaller, closer summit on your right called the Nebel Horn. Head west along the saddle and follow the sharp incline up though the forest, perhaps using your hands to overcome a couple of the more abrupt sections. In the winter and spring, this section of the trail can be slippery. After an aspen grove, the trail winds its way to the western side of the summit ridge and pops out of the trees, just 100 feet shy of the top. Follow the trail up rocky plates, then scramble along the solid ridge to the peak's capstone.

After taking in the view, return to the signpost at the bottom of the summit ridge, then drop down to the west on the West Ridge Trail. If you have the time, head left just beneath the summit for 0.7 mile to South Boulder Peak, the highest peak in Boulder's foothills. Continue down steep talus and notice that the sandstone suddenly gives way to granite.

Amble 1.8 miles down the pleasant, pine-studded ridge, taking in the Indian Peaks views, to intersect the Bear Canyon Trail. Turn right and follow the creek downhill. Some of the rocks at the stream crossings can be slippery. At the bottom of the canyon, you'll pass a fenced power pole and then link up with the Mesa Trail. Go downhill to retrace your path to NCAR.

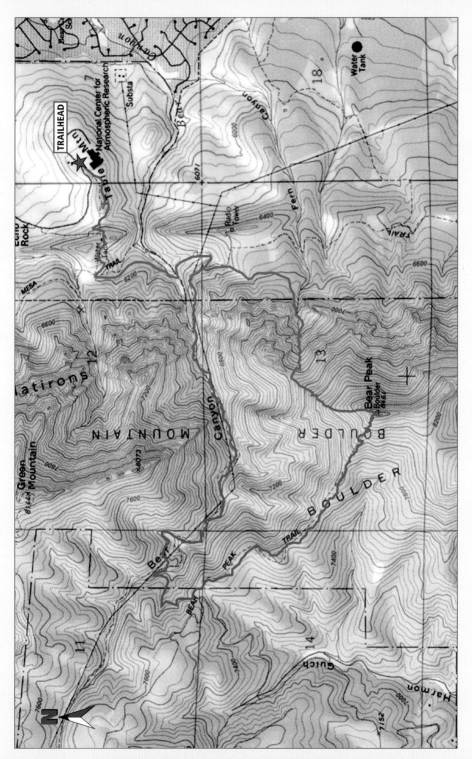

BEAR PEAK LOOP VIA FERN CANYON AND WEST RIDGE

25. Black Lake

BY JAMES RIBNIKER

MAPS	Trails Illustrated, Rocky Mountain National Park, Number 200
	Trails Illustrated, Longs Peak/Bear Lake/Wild Basin/Rocky Mountain National Park, Number 301
	USGS, McHenrys Peak, 7.5 minute
ELEVATION GAIN	1,755 feet; Starting Elevation: 9,242 feet at Glacier Gorge Trailhead
RATING	Easy to Alberta Falls, moderate to Mills Lake, difficult to Black Lake
ROUND-TRIP DISTANCE	8.4 miles to Black Lake
ROUND-TRIP TIME	6–8 hours.
NEAREST LANDMARK	Estes Park

COMMENT: Hiking to Black Lake provides an opportunity to enjoy many of the wonderful sights of Rocky Mountain National Park. The trail is abundant with wildflowers, aspen groves, mountain vistas, marshes, wetlands, lakes, and waterfalls. You'll hike past Alberta Falls, Glacier Falls, and Ribbon Falls. The larger lakes along the trail include Mills Lake, Jewel Lake, and, of course, Black Lake. You will also hike on a variety of terrain, from rocky trails, gravel, and large boulder formations, to split-log paths, large and small bridges, stepping-stone walkways, and rising rock stairways. Sturdy, comfortable hiking boots are highly recommended.

The hike begins at the Glacier Gorge Trailhead and ends high above Black Lake. You will return along the same route. The Glacier Gorge Trailhead is very popular because it provides access to many different trails. Consequently, the small parking lot fills up very early. If the lot is full, park at the Glacier Basin Park 'n' Ride, hop aboard the Bear Lake shuttle bus, and get off at Glacier Gorge Junction. The bus runs from June through September, 7 a.m. until 7 p.m., and the ride is free. You can also ride the shuttle to Bear Lake and hike to the Alberta Falls junction. This 0.4-mile downhill walk is a good warm-up. Check with the ranger at the park entrance for shuttle bus information.

The trail to Black Lake meets with other trails in the park, so it is important to be mindful of your destination. You will pass the trail junctions for Sprague Lake, Bear Lake, Boulder Brook, Lake Haiyaha, and The Loch. Be sure to navigate them correctly. Although the trails are well maintained and marked,

Black Lake.

bring a map. Park maps are available at the park entrance station; consider carrying topographic maps as well.

GETTING THERE: Take U.S. 36 west from Estes Park to the Beaver Meadows Entrance of Rocky Mountain National Park. After entering the park, turn left onto Bear Lake Road and drive to the Park 'n' Ride to catch the shuttle bus, or continue on to the Glacier Gorge Junction or Bear Lake parking lots.

THE ROUTE: From Glacier Gorge, locate the trailhead and follow the trail signs to Mills Lake. From Bear Lake, turn left soon after the Emerald Lake trailhead sign and follow the trail to Alberta Falls. There will be no reference to Black Lake on any of the trail signs until the trail junction with Loch Vale and Lake Haiyaha. Keep left at this junction to continue on to Mills Lake, Jewel Lake, and Black Lake. From the trail past Jewel Lake, look across Glacier Creek where the creek and trail meet and notice the many waterfalls high on the mountainside.

Take the rock staircase alongside Ribbon Falls to reach Black Lake. You may have to use your hands to negotiate a large rock at the top of the falls. When you get to the lake, walk on the rocks until you reach the trail on the lake shore. Continue around the lake and climb the trail along the creek that feeds Black Lake. The trail ends at 11,000 feet, and you can return by simply retracing your steps. If you wish, you can scramble upward among the rocks and continue on to other destinations, such as Blue Lake, Green Lake, or Frozen Lake.

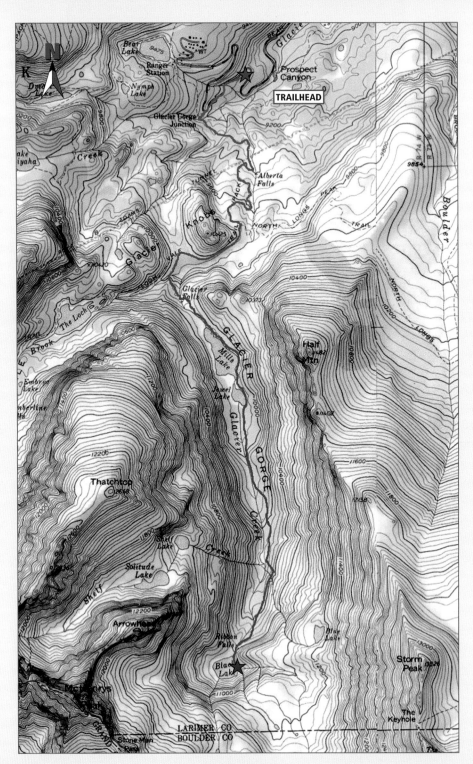

BLACK LAKE

26. Blue Lake

BY DON WALKER

MAPS	Trails Illustrated, Indian Peaks/Gold Hill, Number 102
	USGS, Ward, 7.5 minute
	Colorado Front Range Recreation Topo Map
	Indian Peaks "Trail Tracks" Hiking Map
	Sky Terrain South Rocky Mountain National Park
	Indian Peaks Wilderness Trails Maps
ELEVATION GAIN	900 feet
RATING	Moderate
ROUND-TRIP DISTANCE	5 miles
ROUND-TRIP TIME	4.5 hours
NEAREST LANDMARK	Brainard Lake

COMMENT: This hike will lead you all the way from the quiet shelter of a subalpine evergreen forest to slightly above timberline, where you can stand in a windswept glacial cirque, listening to the roaring sounds of a picturesque waterfall as snowmelt from mighty Mount Toll cascades into the uncanny deep blue water of this high alpine lake. The best time to do this hike, without using snowshoes or other heavy winter gear, is between late June and early October.

GETTING THERE: The drive takes about one hour from Boulder. Take Colorado 119 west to Nederland, and then follow Colorado 72 north just past Ward, turning west onto the Brainard Lake road. After paying the entrance fee, continue and bear right just past Brainard Lake, all the way to the Mitchell Lake/Mt. Audubon Trailhead parking area. Notice that *two* trailheads are situated at this parking area; you will start at the Mitchell Lake Trailhead.

THE ROUTE: The Mitchell Lake Trail starts out as a gentle walk through shady glades of Englemann spruce and other stately conifers. You will reach Mitchell Lake itself in 1.0 mile. Beyond this point, especially if it is early in the hiking season, be prepared to cross a few snowfields.

Beyond Mitchell Lake, the trail opens up and gets steeper. The next 1.5 miles takes you past lovely alpine meadows with, depending upon the time of year, many colorful wildflowers, such as marsh marigolds, columbines, alpine avens, and delicate moss gentian. In this area, some parts of the trail may be wet and muddy, especially during the early half of summer. To avoid increasing erosion, stay on the main trail rather than veering off and destroying vegetation.

Mount Toll presiding over Blue Lake.

PHOTO BY DON WALKER

The closer you get to Blue Lake, the more expansive the views become. In the final 0.5 mile, you will find yourself on the east side of a glacial valley and see runoff from Blue Lake in the creek below you. At this point, you will begin to leave the taller trees behind you, and soon the trail is edged with *krummholz*—dwarf trees twisted into gnarled shapes by severe weather conditions. By the time you reach the lake, the trail is mostly rock and you will notice occasional piles of smaller rocks—cairns—made by hikers to mark the trail.

Blue Lake is one of the most spectacular places in the Indian Peaks Wilderness. Sitting at an elevation of 11,338 feet and covering more than 20 acres, the lake is said to be over 100 feet deep at the center. The striking dark blue color of the water is attributed to minerals pulverized by the glacier that once stood on top of the lake. Due west of the lake and forming part of the Continental Divide, nearly pyramidal Mount Toll rises to a stately 12,979 feet, dramatically dominating the skyline. On the opposite shore directly below Toll is a waterfall that you can see and hear clearly from anywhere near the lake. You will find plenty of huge rocks along the shoreline, offering both shelter from the wind and nice places to sit and eat your picnic lunch. Return by retracing your steps.

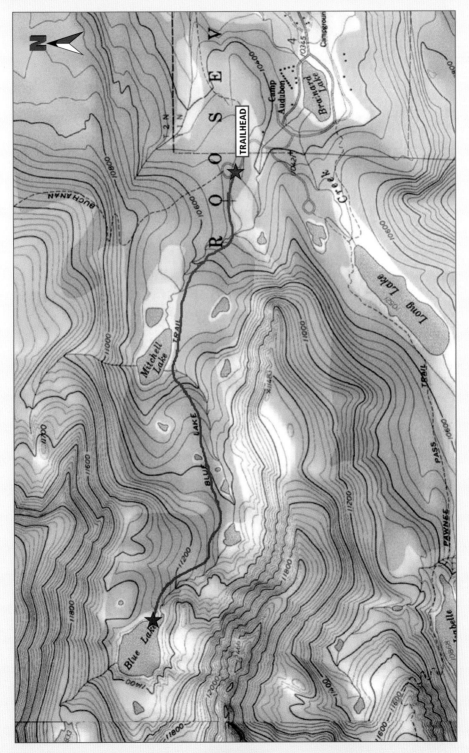

BLUE LAKE

27. Diamond Lake

BY STEVE HORACE

MAPS	Trails Illustrated, Indian Peaks/Gold Hill, Number 102 USGS, Nederland, Monarch Lake, and East Portal, 7.5 minute
ELEVATION GAIN	840 feet
RATING	Moderate
ROUND-TRIP DISTANCE	4.6 miles
ROUND-TRIP TIME	3 hours
NEAREST LANDMARK	Arapaho Pass

COMMENT: You start to hear it soon after leaving the trailhead: an ever-increasing roar of water in the distance. Then you see it—a spectacular cascade of waterfalls thundering down the mountain across the valley. Let your eyes follow it up: that's where you are going—this cascade flows from Diamond Lake.

The Diamond Lake Trail offers a superb high-altitude, summertime, family hike. This well-maintained U.S. Forest Service trail features outstanding scenery, gentle grades, cascading streams, and a dizzying array of summer wildflowers. The trail starts above 10,000 feet, so be prepared for cool and changeable weather conditions.

GETTING THERE: From Boulder, head up Boulder Canyon to Nederland, then go south (left) on Colorado 72 for about 0.6 mile. Turn right on County Road 130 toward Eldora. Stay right where the road forks for Eldora Ski Area. Go through the little town of Eldora, after which the road turns to dirt. Proceed past the Hessie Trailhead, stay right and continue for 4.0 miles on the dirt road to the parking lot on the right for the Fourth of July Trailhead, which is adjacent to the Buckingham Campground. A high-clearance vehicle is useful for reaching this popular entry into the Indian Peaks Wilderness Area.

THE ROUTE: Take the Arapaho Pass Trail as it contours up through the forest and opens to some impressive views of the Middle Boulder Creek valley and surrounding peaks. Cross some small tumbling streams as you traverse northwest up the valley, then cross a larger stream on well-placed stepping stones. Go left at the marked trail intersection at about the 1.0-mile point, where the Diamond Lake Trail splits off from the Arapaho Pass Trail. The Diamond Lake Trail gradually descends to Middle Boulder Creek, where

Diamond Lake from above.

PHOTO BY STEVE HORACE

a log bridge with a handrail will assist your crossing. The trail turns back to the southeast and starts a gradual ascent through forests and flower-filled bogs with log walkways. Near Diamond Lake, there is a marked trail intersection at which the Diamond Lake Trail continues to the left, but go right, toward the camping areas, and soon Diamond Lake will appear. The lake sits just below treeline, at 10,940 feet. Hike around the right side of the lake to view the tumbling, braided inlet stream and surrounding wildflowers. Camping is available at the lake, in designated campsites. Permits are required to camp here in the summer.

SIDEBAR: SOME ADDITIONAL FUN

For the more adventurous, you can follow faint trails and the inlet streams for another mile to Upper Diamond Lake, which sits well above treeline, at 11,800 feet, in an impressive mountain cirque. Turn right after reaching Diamond Lake, follow the lakeside trail and cross the first inlet stream. Continue to near the second inlet stream, follow it up past a small lake and ascend northwest, past a rocky rise on your right, to Upper Diamond Lake. Some faint trails may assist in the effort, but the ascent is relatively straight-forward and the main challenge is skirting the bogs scattered along the way. Substantial snowfields may linger and the upper lake may stay frozen through late summer. Returning is relatively easy, as impressive views of Diamond Lake are available for most of the descent.

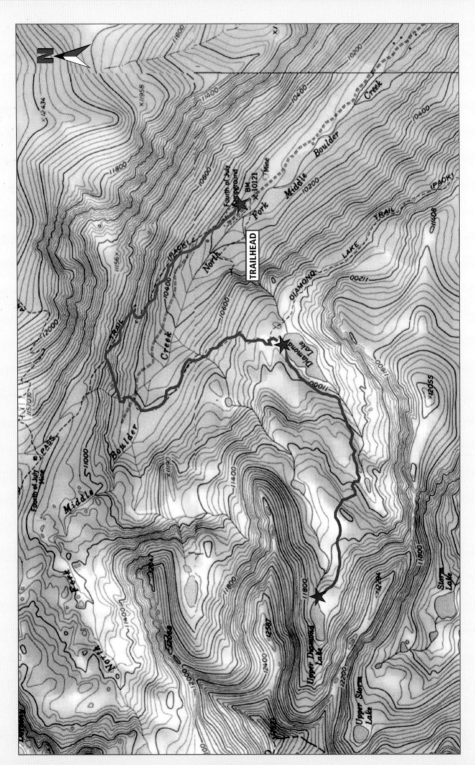

DIAMOND LAKE

28. Eldorado Canyon Trail

BY JANINE FUGERE

MAPS	Trails Illustrated, Boulder/Golden, Number 100
	USGS, Eldorado Springs, 7.5 Minute
	CMC Trail Map, Boulder Mountain Parks and Nearby
	Open Space
ELEVATION GAIN	1,381 feet
RATING	Moderate–difficult
ROUND-TRIP DISTANCE	7 miles
ROUND-TRIP TIME	3.5 hours
NEAREST LANDMARK	Eldorado Springs

COMMENT: This lovely trail in Eldorado Canyon State Park makes it hard to believe that you are close to Boulder and Denver. There are stunning views of Eldorado Canyon and the Continental Divide, steep ascents and descents, rolling strolls through lush, densely wooded areas, huge lichen-covered boulders, and plentiful wildflowers. The trail begins and ends near South Boulder Creek, which carved Eldorado Canyon.

GETTING THERE: In Boulder, from Broadway and Table Mesa, go 2.7 miles south on Colorado 93 to Colorado 170. Turn right. (From Denver, take Interstate 25 north, then U.S. 36 west to the Louisville-Superior exit. Turn left on McCaslin Boulevard, cross U.S. 36, and then turn right onto Colorado 170. Go 4.3 miles west on Colorado 170 and cross Colorado 93.) From the light at Colorado 93 and Colorado 170, go 3.3 miles west on Colorado 170 to the park entrance. A day-use fee or an Annual Colorado State Parks Pass is required to enter. Go another 0.7 mile, then over a small bridge and veer left to the Visitor Center. Park in the nearby lot.

THE ROUTE: Near the Visitor Center, a large sign marks the start of the Eldorado Canyon Trail. A set of steps leads up to the right and goes across a dirt service road to more steps. You will encounter obvious social trails and marked restoration areas, so stay on the main trail.

The trail begins with a series of switchbacks that offer views of the opposite side of the canyon, including a train track high on the south canyon wall. Finally, the high peaks of the Continental Divide become visible to the west. The trail then wanders through pines and boulders.

Next, the trail heads into boulder fields, and seems to disappear, but you'll

Morning light on the Eldorado Canyon Trail.

find a place to cross these boulders on small rocks. Now, a moderate climb begins with some big steps, more switchbacks, and better views of the Continental Divide. When you cross a smooth ledge, you're almost at the same elevation as the train tracks across the canyon.

The trail eases down into a draw through trees, moss, giant ferns, and wildflowers. This area has some gigantic boulders and it's hard to imagine how they stay so precariously balanced. Descend into the woods, pass some area closure signs, and then go across a small wooden footbridge. A moderate uphill climb leads to a ridge crest with good views. The trail turns west and leads to another ridge crest before the final steep descent into Martin Gulch. Some people turn around here rather than go all the way down, only to have to climb back up. If you continue, the trail comes to the bottom of a small ravine, easily crossed by stepping on logs. Soon you'll start to hear the sound of South Boulder Creek. Continue downhill, switching back and forth toward the creek. A sharp switchback to the right brings you to the end of the trail, where it intersects the Walker Ranch Loop Trail. A worthwhile side trip is to follow that trail about 0.1 mile to the left, across a bridge over South Boulder Creek, to a small waterfall upstream.

SIDEBAR: CONEY ISLAND OF THE WEST

Eldorado Canyon is rich in history. Ute Indians originally settled it, then settlers came in the 1850s. In the early 1900s, Eldorado Springs became a booming hot springs resort, known as "The Coney Island of the West," and attracted visitors from all over the world seeking a respite from urban life. In the resort's heyday, a far more spectacular view than the railroad was visible while gazing across the canyon: Daredevil Ivy Baldwin would walk a 582-foot-high tightrope, 635 feet across the canyon, without a net below him. Baldwin made his daring crossing 89 times starting in 1907, and made his last crossing in 1948 at the age of 82.

The railroad cut across the valley from the Eldorado Canyon Trail.   PHOTO BY JANINE FUGERE

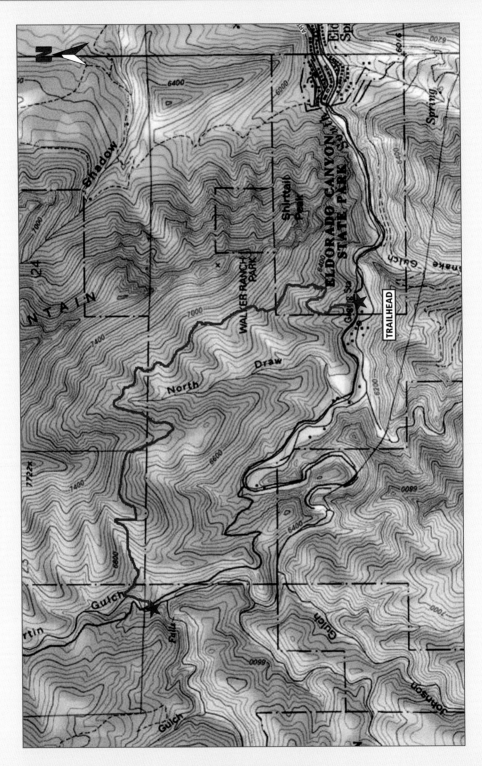

ELDORADO CANYON TRAIL

29. Green Mountain via Gregory Canyon

BY ROBERT ROOT

MAPS	Trails Illustrated, Boulder/Golden, Number 100
	USGS, Eldorado Springs, 7.5 Minute
	CMC Trail Map, Boulder Mountain Parks and Nearby
	Open Space
ELEVATION GAIN	2,344 feet
RATING	Moderate–difficult
ROUND-TRIP DISTANCE	6 miles
ROUND-TRIP TIME	3–4 hours
NEAREST LANDMARK	Boulder

COMMENT: Green Mountain is an accessible summit that provides views of Boulder and the plains in one direction, and the high peaks of the Continental Divide in the other. Several intersecting trails offer a variety of loops and possibilities for shortening or lengthening the hike.

GETTING THERE: In Boulder, go west on Baseline Road from the intersection with Broadway, past the turnoff for Chautauqua Park. Cautiously turn left where Baseline becomes Flagstaff Mountain Road and drive to the Gregory Canyon Trailhead. This small, often-crowded parking lot is a fee area for non–Boulder County residents. Arrive early or expect to have to park along the road and walk back to the trailhead. Parking near Chautauqua Park adds another 0.7 mile to your hike.

THE ROUTE: From the Gregory Canyon Trailhead, follow the Gregory Canyon Trail west, at first paralleling, then rising above Gregory Creek. Stay right at the intersection with the Saddle Rock Trail. The trail is verdant at first, then becomes a steep, steady uphill climb on a rocky path.

   The narrow, rocky trail gains 900 feet in 1.0 mile and levels out at the top of a ridge, where the undergrowth thickens again. The trail is wider and easier for about 0.2 mile, where a trail marker indicates the end of the Gregory Canyon Trail and the beginning of the Ranger Trail. The Green Mountain Lodge, a stone cabin built by the Civilian Conservation Corps (CCC) during the Great Depression, is located here, as well as a restroom, picnic area, and the junction with the Long Canyon Trail. (For a shorter hike, this is a good place to turn around.) Head left of the lodge and follow the Ranger Trail south through

Green Mountain at first light.

thick woods, on a wide, easy, uphill trail that will reach the junction with the E. M. Greenman Trail, an alternative route to the summit, or a possible return route from it. Stay on the Ranger Trail, which becomes steeper and narrower as it ascends the northwestern slope of Green Mountain.

The Ranger Trail gains another 1,190 feet in 1.1 miles and ends at the junction of the Green Bear Trail and the Green Mountain West Ridge Trail. Turn left onto the Green Mountain Trail and begin a 0.2-mile ascent to the summit of Green Mountain (8,144 feet). This section of the trail passes through more open, rocky terrain and is the most strenuous portion of the hike. The loose scree on the trail can make for tricky traction. The trail goes up a log step, turns left, and the summit appears as a large boulder with a cemented stone cairn on top of it. On top of the cairn is a metal disc that helps identify the peaks in the distance to the west. The summit takes a little rock scrambling to reach and can be crowded if several people are on it.

The simplest return route is down the Green Mountain West Ridge Trail to the intersection with the Ranger Trail. An alternative route is to go off the summit to the north on the E. M. Greenman Trail. This is a steeper descent that adds 0.4 mile to the hike. It will circle around to intersect the Ranger Trail for the hike back down to the Green Mountain Lodge and the Gregory Canyon Trailhead.

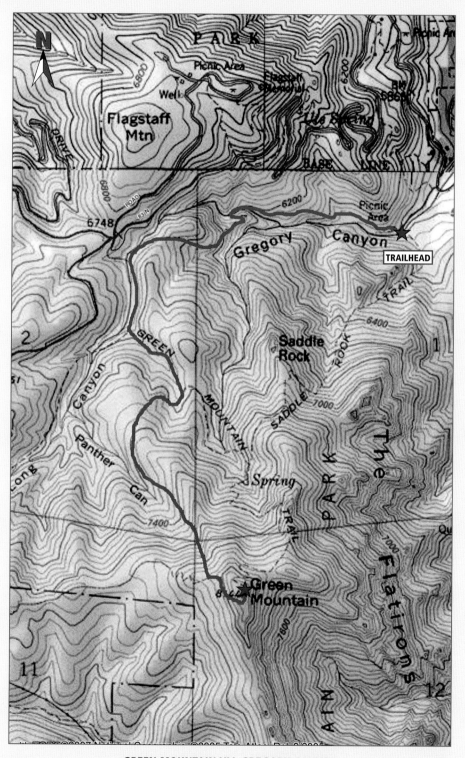

GREEN MOUNTAIN VIA GREGORY CANYON

30. Heart Lake

BY TERRIE HARDIE

MAPS	Trails Illustrated, Winter Park/Central City/Rollins Pass, Number 103
	USGS, East Portal, 7.5 minute
ELEVATION GAIN	2,100 feet
RATING	Moderate
ROUND-TRIP DISTANCE	8.4 miles
ROUND-TRIP TIME	4 hours in summer; 6 hours or more in winter
NEAREST LANDMARK	Rollinsville

COMMENT: Take this hike for the great views of the high peaks and abundant wildflowers that surround these two alpine lakes. We say two lakes because the re-routed trail passes Rogers Pass Lake on the way to Heart Lake. Most trail maps still show the trail going directly to Heart Lake, but because of deadfalls and severe erosion, that trail is obscured and is no longer maintained by the Forest Service. Heart Lake and Rogers Pass Lake are in the James Peak Wilderness, which was established in 2002. Heart Lake gets its name from its heart shape.

GETTING THERE: From Boulder, take Colorado 119 (Canyon Blvd.) west to Nederland. At the traffic circle, go left (south) on Colorado 72 to Rollinsville. Turn right on County Road 16, which follows the railroad tracks, west past the town of Tolland, to the East Portal railroad tunnel. Park on the left side of the road, next to the tracks.

Alternatively, if you're coming from the Denver-Golden area, go north on Colorado 93 to the intersection with Colorado 72. Turn left and follow the road west along Coal Creek to the intersection with Colorado 119. Turn left and go to Rollinsville. Turn right on County Road 16 and go past Tolland to the East Portal railroad tunnel. Park on the left side of the road, next to the tracks.

THE ROUTE: From the East Portal Trailhead parking area, cross the road and start at the trail sign for the James Peak Wilderness Access. After a short distance, you will pass a sign with useful information about the trails in this area and regulations for wilderness travel. The wilderness boundary is another 100 feet up the trail. The trail passes an old cabin on the left as it continues west through a thick forest of mostly spruce trees.

Rogers Pass Lake on the way to Heart Lake.

Cross three footbridges built by volunteers from the Colorado Mountain Club. After about 1.0 mile, there is a clearing where the trail to Forest and Arapaho lakes takes off to the right. Continue straight, past some old cabin remains, as you begin to gain elevation. A series of switchbacks was built by Wildlands Restoration Volunteers to improve this section of the trail. The trail passes a sign on the right for the trail to Crater Lakes, which is sometimes obscured by foliage. The trail then winds along the South Boulder Creek drainage, crossing it several times.

It can be a challenge to stay on this trail in winter, as there are few markers to show the way. After crossing a log footbridge, the trail gets much steeper before the final approach to Rogers Pass Lake. There is a meadow before the lake, with several side trails. The main trail continues straight west toward the Continental Divide (Note: the area below Rogers Pass Lake may have snow drifts well into late spring and early summer, followed by very wet conditions as the snow melts). Continue around the north side of Rogers Pass Lake, where the trail climbs to the top of a ridge. Near the top of the ridge, the trail splits. The right branch goes to Heart Lake, where you'll find a weathered wooden sign with the lake's name barely visible. The left branch goes to Rogers Pass on the Continental Divide. Here you can pick up the Continental Divide Trail and take it south to the summit of James Peak.

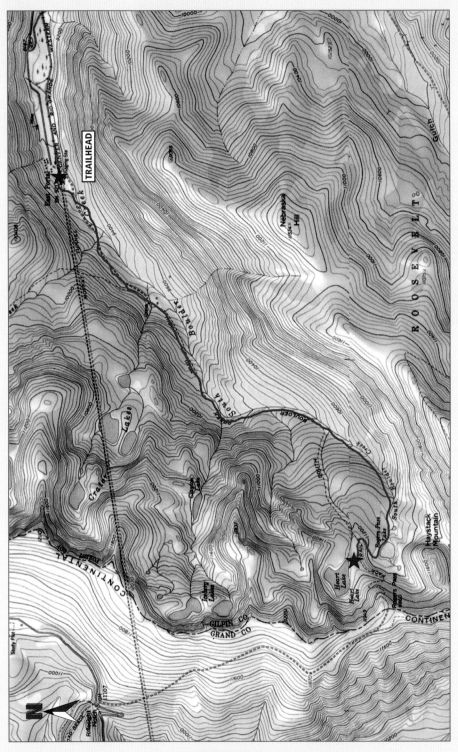

HEART LAKE

31. Meadow Mountain and St. Vrain Mountain

BY NEAL ZAUN

MAPS	Trails Illustrated, Rocky Mountain National Park, Number 200 USGS, Allenspark, 7.5 minute
ELEVATION GAIN	Meadow Mountain: 2,650 feet St. Vrain Mountain: 3,180 feet (Combined: 3,610 feet)
RATING	Moderate–difficult
ROUND-TRIP DISTANCE	Meadow Mountain: 6.6 miles St. Vrain Mountain: 8.6 miles (Combined: 9.2 miles)
ROUND-TRIP TIME	Combined: 7 hours
NEAREST LANDMARK	Allenspark

COMMENT: This trail provides one of the most panoramic views of the high peaks in the Wild Basin region of Rocky Mountain National Park. Directly to the north are 13,911-foot Mount Meeker and 14,256-foot Longs Peak. The trip allows some choice of difficulty and provides more solitude than most hikes. Sections of the trail pass through both the Indian Peaks Wilderness Area and the southern edge of Rocky Mountain National Park. Meadow Mountain is named for the large alpine tundra meadow just below it, which is full of alpine flowers from late June to early August. To avoid much snow, hike after mid-June.

GETTING THERE: Drive north from Boulder on U.S. 36 for about 14 miles, to the town of Lyons. At the west end of Lyons, turn left on Colorado 7 and head toward Allenspark. At Allenspark, take the second exit into town. After this "main" street curves left, turn right on Ski Road (County Road 107). This gravel road winds between houses, then heads straight south for 1.6 miles to a split in the road. Go to the right for 0.5 mile to the St. Vrain Trailhead parking lot. The other road goes to the former Rock Creek Ski Area, which was popular from 1947 to the early 1950s. In the winter, the road is usually plowed to the split, providing access to the valley for snow-shoeing and backcountry skiing.

THE ROUTE: The trail is laid out to provide a steady, moderate elevation gain

Longs Peak peeks through the clouds at the Meadow–St. Vrain saddle.

throughout the entire trail. From the trailhead, the trail heads directly west through a lodgepole pine and aspen forest for about 1.0 mile. The trail stays to the north of the stream, which runs until the higher snow has completely melted, in about mid-July. At the head of the valley, the trees change to a spruce and fir forest and the trail has a large switchback to ease the grade up to the saddle. In the trees, there are usually some snowdrifts until the end of June; these are consolidated enough to walk over. Just before the top of the saddle, the trees give way to large bushes called *krummholz,* which is German for crooked or bent wood. They are stunted by the high winds and cold and are often very old.

After you break out of the trees and start to head west-southwest, Meadow Mountain is on the right, directly north. There is no trail to the top. Simply scramble up the boulder field for about 0.3 mile with an elevation gain of 400 feet. From the top of Meadow Mountain, St. Vrain Mountain, or the saddle, there is a panoramic view of the mountains surrounding the Wild Basin Area. In the Wild Basin valley bottom you can still see the remnants of the 1978 Ouzel Fire. The fire started from a lightning strike at the valley's west end and spread to within 1.0 mile of Allenspark before being extinguished.

To climb St. Vrain Mountain, start at the saddle, then go southwest for about 0.5 mile until you are directly to the east of the mountain, near the Rocky Mountain National Park sign. From here, go directly west, first through a few patches of krummholz, and then on to the top for an elevation gain of 950 feet. Before mid-July there will be some snow, and ski poles may help your stability. St. Vrain Mountain is named after Ceran St. Vrain, a trapper and trader who roamed Colorado and New Mexico in the mid-1800s.

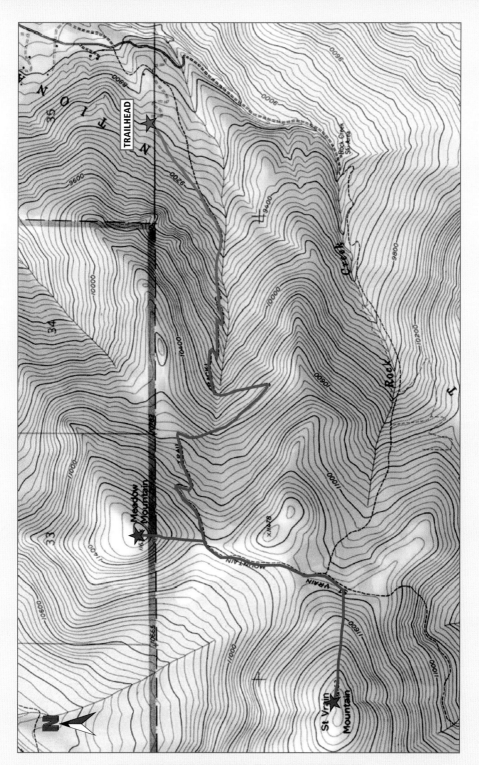

MEADOW MOUNTAIN AND ST. VRAIN MOUNTAIN

32. Mesa Trail

BY ART ROBERTS

MAPS	Trails Illustrated, Boulder/Golden, Number 100 USGS, Eldorado Springs, 7.5 minute CMC Trail Map, Boulder Mountain Parks and Nearby Open Space Boulder Open Space and Mountain Parks Trails Map
ELEVATION GAIN	Minus 329 (not counting many ups and downs)
RATING	Easy
ROUND-TRIP DISTANCE	13.8 miles
ROUND-TRIP TIME	5–5.5 hours
NEAREST LANDMARK	Boulder

COMMENT: The Mesa Trail is the central artery of one of the finest hiking trail systems in the country, and it is the pride of Boulder. The Mesa Trail itself is almost 7 miles long as it stretches between Boulder and Eldorado Springs. Twenty-one other named trails originate from it; all are delightful.

Many parts of this area are habitat conservation areas, created to protect the many species of wildlife that live here. Please observe all closure and dog control signs.

GETTING THERE: The Mesa Trail is accessible from Chautauqua Park, the National Center for Atmospheric Research (NCAR), and from the south trailhead near Eldorado Springs. Chautauqua Park is just south of Baseline Road and 8th Street in Boulder. NCAR is at the west end of Table Mesa Drive. From Broadway, turn west onto Table Mesa Drive and drive to its end. Park and hike west to intersect with the Mesa Trail. To get to the south trailhead, drive south on Broadway to Colorado 170, turn west toward Eldorado Springs, go 1.6 miles and turn right at the trailhead sign.

THE ROUTE: The easiest access to the Mesa Trail is from Chautauqua Park. The OSMP 2008 trails map shows the Mesa Trail starting at the Visitor Center, so measure distances from here. Hike up the Bluebell road 0.5 mile to the well-marked intersection with the Mesa Trail. Leave the road here and continue on the Mesa Trail, past the Enchanted Mesa Trail at 1.0 mile, and the Kohler Mesa Trail at 1.1 miles. Notice Skunk Canyon, ahead and to your left, and the NCAR research facility farther south. Proceed to the Skunk Canyon Trail intersection at 1.5 miles. There are good views to the east from here.

Paradise, one half hour from Boulder—Green Mountain from the southeast. PHOTO BY ART ROBERTS

As you continue, see if you can spot Bear Peak to the southwest. Intersect with the NCAR Trail at 2.0 miles. The Mallory Cave Trail also starts here. Intersect with an access road at 2.4 miles, with the Bear Canyon kiosk on your right. Continue past the kiosk to the Bear Canyon Trail at 2.7 miles. This trail leads to the west ridges of Bear Peak and Green Mountain.

The Fern Canyon Trail, at mile 2.9, leads to the north side of Bear Peak. About 500 feet up from the Fern Canyon trail, leave the access road and turn south at another kiosk. At mile 3.4, intersect the North Fork of the Shanahan Trail. Proceed to mile 3.9, to the South Fork of the Shanahan Trail. The Shanahan trails make for a great loop addition to your hike. Proceed to the Big Bluestem Trail, at 4.3 miles.

Next are trails at 4.5 and 4.9 miles that take you to Shadow Canyon. These are also good for a short side trip. As the trail starts to descend, note the views, opening up to the southeast, of Doudy Draw, Greenbelt Plateau, and Marshall Mesa. The next intersection is with the main Shadow Canyon Trail, at mile 5.2. Continue down the access road to intersect with the Towhee Trail at 5.6 miles, Big Bluestem Trail at 5.9, South Boulder Creek Trail at 6.1, Towhee, again, at 6.3, and Towhee/Homestead at 6.7 miles. Cross South Boulder Creek on a bridge and end at the parking lot.

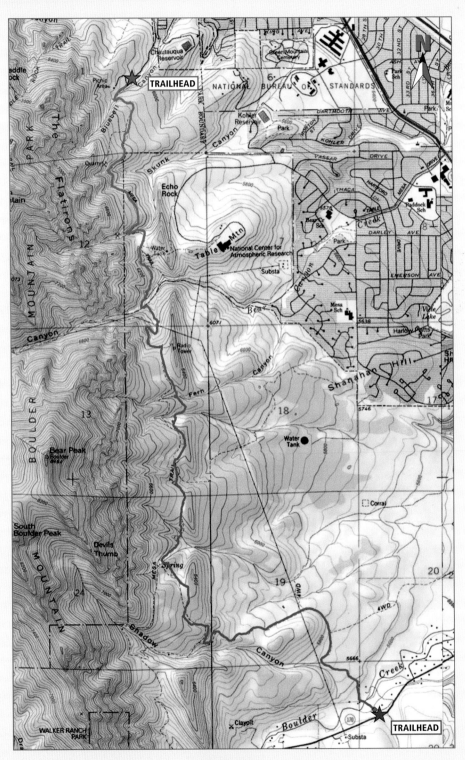

MESA TRAIL

33. Mount Audubon

BY DARYL OGDEN

MAPS	Trails Illustrated, Indian Peaks/Gold Hill, Number 102 USGS, Ward, 7.5 minute
ELEVATION GAIN	2,825 feet
RATING	Moderate
ROUND-TRIP DISTANCE	7.5 miles
ROUND TRIP TIME	4–5 hours
NEAREST LANDMARK	Ward

COMMENT: Colorado boasts more than 750 peaks with elevations between 13,000 feet and 14,000 feet above sea level. Mount Audubon rises 13,223 feet in the Roosevelt National Forest, west of Boulder. This well-marked trail passes through subalpine forest and beautifully austere alpine tundra. The peak was named for John James Audubon, the nineteenth-century painter famous for producing portraits of birds and mammals. Although he never visited Colorado, Audubon has thus been honored for his contributions to an awareness of our nation's natural heritage.

GETTING THERE: Drive north out of Boulder on Foothills Highway for 4.5 miles to the Jamestown turnoff. Travel west about 5 miles to the Ward turnoff, on the left, and continue 12 miles through that tiny town. Turn right onto Colorado 72 (the Peak-to-Peak Highway) for about 50 yards, then left at the Brainard Lake Recreational Area sign. About 2.7 miles up the road, stop and pay the entrance fee. Go another 3 miles, pass Brainard Lake, and follow signs to the Mitchell Lake parking lot, where the road ends.

THE ROUTE: Begin the hike at the Mount Audubon-Buchanan Pass Trailhead, in the northwest corner of the parking lot. The trail climbs steadily through a heavily wooded subalpine forest of Engelmann spruce, subalpine fir, and lodgepole pine. As late as early July, shaded areas of the trail can still have patches of deep snow. Several switchbacks ease the climb as the trail passes through the transitional zone that marks the boundary between the forest and the treeless alpine tundra. Krummholz characterizes this zone. The eastern face of Mount Audubon looms as you exit the trees.

At 1.5 miles into the hike, the trail splits at a weathered wooden marker pointing the way to the Buchanan Pass Trail to the north and to the remaining 2 miles westward to the saddle at the base of Mount Audubon.

Mount Audubon from Brainard Lake.

The hike from here crosses wide-open, rocky terrain dotted with purple alpine gentian, blue forget-me-nots, red king's crown, and the impressive white circles of the alpine spring beauty. Yellow-bellied marmots, chirping pikas, and the grouse-like ptarmigan, with its seasonally camouflaged feathers, are among the few permanent residents of the tundra.

There are various routes through the rocks and boulders that make up the last 625 feet of the climb from the saddle to the summit, some marked by small cairns. This final push of the hike is strenuous, but the rewards are incredible when you stand on the top. Expansive vistas stretch from the far plains in the east to the edge of Rocky Mountain National Park in the west, and beyond. Longs Peak sits to the north, and the Indian Peaks, Mount Toll, and faraway Mount Evans are visible to the south.

The vertical drops surrounding the summit are precipitous, with the dark Coney and Upper Coney lakes visible almost 2,500 feet below on the north side. Lake Granby in the Frazier valley can be seen in the west. The summit has several rock-walled dugouts in which to hide from the wind and relax while you enjoy this wondrous location.

Exhilaration on the summit.

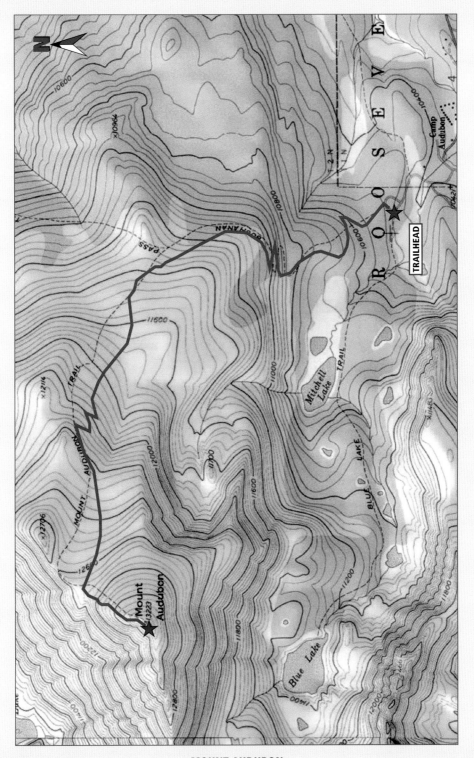

MOUNT AUDUBON

34. Mount Sanitas

BY MARILYN FELLOWS

MAPS	Trails Illustrated, Boulder/Golden, Number 100 USGS, Boulder, 7.5 minute CMC Trail Map, Boulder Mountain Parks and Nearby Open Space
ELEVATION GAIN	1,300 feet
RATING	Moderate–difficult
ROUND-TRIP DISTANCE	2.8 miles (3.3 miles for the loop)
ROUND-TRIP TIME	2–2.5 hours
NEAREST LANDMARK	Mapleton Medical Center

COMMENT: Mount Sanitas offers spectacular vistas of the city and plains to the east as well as views of the Continental Divide to the west. The trail can be hiked most of the year and it offers different attractions depending upon the season. Wildflowers abound from May to July, including penstemon, cinquefoil, western spiderwort, and evening primrose.

You'll never be lonely on this popular hike: be prepared to share the trail with lots of folks and lots of dogs. If you want your dogs along, read the leash laws at the trailhead. There is little shade on the trail, so wear a hat and sunglasses, use sunscreen, and bring at least a liter of water. During the cooler months, bring extra clothing to ward off the wind, and always wear sturdy hiking shoes.

GETTING THERE: Take Mapleton Avenue west from Broadway and go past the Mapleton Medical Center. There are two small parking areas on the right (north), and one farther along on the left. If those lots are full, try farther back along Mapleton. The lots fill early, especially on weekends, so try to arrive before 8 a.m. Trailheads for both Mount Sanitas and Sanitas Valley are just north of the parking areas.

THE ROUTE: Mount Sanitas can be climbed two ways—via the Sanitas Valley Trail, then turning west onto the steep East Ridge Trail; or by hiking the Mount Sanitas Trail itself. From the summit, you can make a loop by descending the East Ridge Trail and returning along the very gentle Sanitas Valley Trail. The latter choice is recommended and is described here.

The first 0.5 mile of the Mount Sanitas Trail is the steepest, and you will be grateful for the occasional flat spots where you can pause and catch your

Even without the sun, a treat—the Sanitas Valley Trail.

breath. Lovely rock formations on the right harbor nesting places for raptors and other birds, and if you are lucky you may see—or at least hear—falcons at play. You'll also pass several favorite bouldering spots where local climbers practice their skills.

The steep, log-reinforced stairs close to the trailhead disappear as the trail opens up to breathtaking views of the plains and the city. You'll see the Sanitas Valley Trail below you, on the right, and have glimpses of the majestic Indian Peaks Wilderness and Continental Divide, on your left. Behind you to the south is the top of the First Flatiron rising above Chautauqua Park, only a few miles away.

The trail continues to hit you with quite steep stretches and, in the final 0.25 mile, you'll reach a steep false summit. Don't lose hope—from here you can see the real summit. Continue through a wooded glade, which hides the steep rocky steps of the last 100 feet to the top. One more short burst, and you're there, 6,800 feet above sea level.

Sit a while on the sandstone rocks and admire the toy-like view of Boulder below and the Great Plains to the east. Notice the surveyor's steel post embedded in the summit rock.

After your rest, decide how to return. If you elect to do the loop, shortly down the east side of the Sanitas summit you'll find a sign pointing the way to the East Ridge Trail. This is an interesting but sometimes confusing path, which winds through a few rock mazes, so pay attention to all the trail markings. When you ultimately reach the valley below, the Sanitas Valley Trail will be obvious, and all that remains is a gentle and pleasant stroll along a wide gravel trail back to the parking areas.

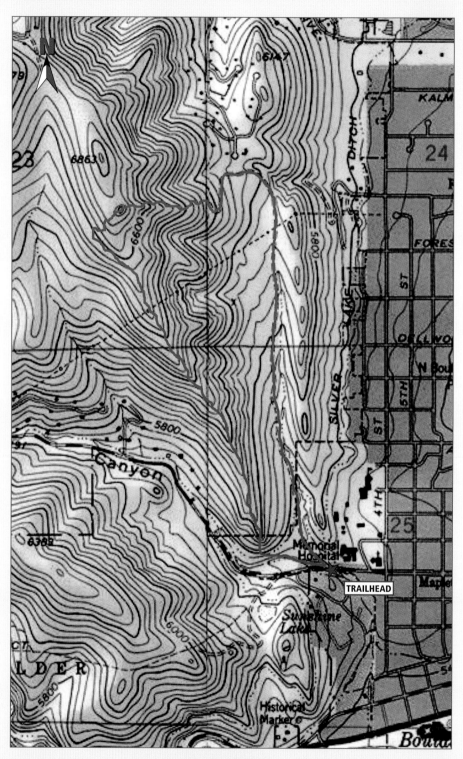

MOUNT SANITAS

35. Pawnee Pass

BY LINCOLN GUP

MAPS	Trails Illustrated, Indian Peaks/Gold Hill, Number 102
	USGS, Ward, 7.5 minute
	USGS, Monarch Lake, 7.5 minute
ELEVATION GAIN	2,419 feet
RATING	Moderate–difficult
ROUND-TRIP DISTANCE	8.6 miles
ROUND-TRIP TIME	7 hours
NEAREST LANDMARK	Brainard Lake

COMMENT: Follow a string of idyllic lakes up a glacier-carved, U-shaped valley before climbing high on the Continental Divide for breathtaking views of numerous rugged peaks. Colorful blooms and birds will escort you to a beautiful lake fed by tumbling glacial streams. The track then zigzags up a series of shelves and meadows to bring you into a rich world of rocks, flowers, and tussock grasses on a high alpine pass.

GETTING THERE: From the intersection of U.S. 36 and Broadway Street in north Boulder, drive north on U.S. 36. At 4.8 miles, turn left onto Lefthand Canyon Drive. Turn left at 5.2 miles to stay on Lefthand Canyon Drive. Go another 11.6 miles, up through the town of Ward to the Peak-to-Peak Highway (Colorado 72). Turn right (north); then take an immediate left onto the Brainard Lake Road. Between June and late fall, pay the entry fee at the winter closure gate, at 2.7 miles, then continue another 3.1 miles to the Long Lake Trailhead. At other times of the year, you must walk from the gate to the trailhead.

THE ROUTE: The Pawnee Pass Trail starts on the south side of the parking lot and immediately enters a dense subalpine forest of pine, fir, and Englemann spruce.

At 0.2 mile, a short walk to the left, along the Jean Lunning Trail, to the Long Lake outlet stream, affords a stunning view across the lake at the towering peaks hemming the source of the South St. Vrain creek. Continue along the Pawnee Pass Trail, parallel to Long Lake's north shore, past marshy areas that sport a palette of arnica, marsh marigold, and rosy paintbrush. Bear right at the second intersection with the Jean Lunning Trail, at 1.2 miles, and continue up the gentle grade for 0.8 mile to Lake Isabelle.

Approaching Lake Isabelle, on the way to Pawnee Peak.

Stop and gape: a dazzling panorama of sharp peaks fills the sky as you arrive on the flower-studded eastern shore slightly above the lake. Two of the peaks—conical Navajo Peak on the left, and its neighbor to the right, Apache Peak, rise above 13,000 feet and harbor visible glaciers on their flanks.

Follow the Pawnee Pass Trail to the north as it climbs alongside a crystalline brook. After about 0.25 mile, cross the first of two wooden footbridges. The trail quickly passes through krummholz and moist meadows before launching steeply skyward on a series of switchbacks.

A precipitous overlook a few feet south of the trail, 1.1 miles beyond Lake Isabelle, affords a spectacular view 900 feet down crumbling, pinkish-gold cliffs to the valley below. Continue on the trail across a rocky bench, and then proceed up through the talus. Several small snowfields below the pass may remain until late summer. Cross these carefully. When you reach the trail sign at Pawnee Pass, you are on the Continental Divide, standing 12,541 feet above sea level.

The fragile tundra here is adorned with ankle-high plants, such as the alpine forget-me-not and queen's crown that have evolved to withstand the cold winds that frequently sweep the pass. If you can afford the time, peer down the western side of the pass to see the 23 precipitous switchbacks descending 1,700 feet to Pawnee Lake, or ascend the steep ridge to the north and follow the cairns for stunning views down three drainages from the summit of Pawnee Peak (12,943 feet). Retrace your steps to return to the trailhead.

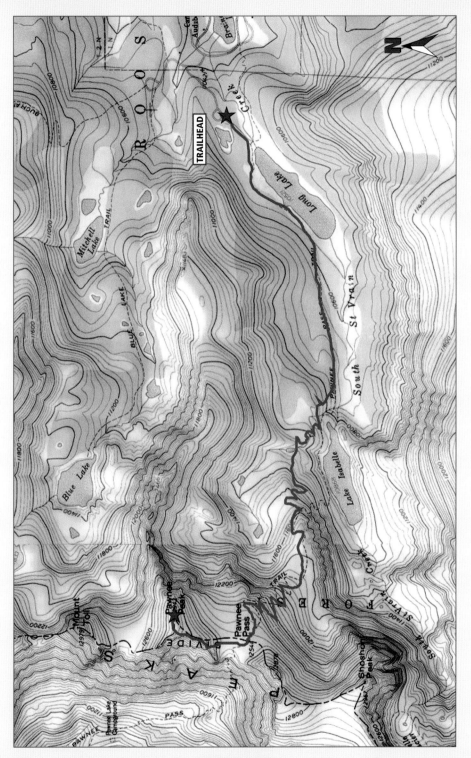

PAWNEE PASS

36. Twin Sisters Peaks

BY ART ROBERTS

MAPS	Trails Illustrated, Longs Peak/Bear Lake/Wild Basin, Number 301
	USGS, Longs Peak, 7.5 minute
ELEVATION GAIN	2,190 feet
RATING	Difficult
ROUND-TRIP DISTANCE	7.4 miles
ROUND-TRIP TIME	4.5–5 hours
NEAREST LANDMARK	Estes Park

COMMENT: This is a great trail for hikers, trail runners, and photographers. The summits are made up of two closely spaced peaks and one more distant mountaintop. Even if you only go to the first, lower, peak, this hike is a rewarding experience. The views from the peaks area, especially of Longs Peak, are outstanding and make this hike a perfect addition to your summer outings.

This area is known for being windy; bring a waterproof windbreaker and extra layers of clothing. The summit area is quite exposed, and you will want to get up and back early to avoid afternoon thunderstorms. Parts of this trail are inside Rocky Mountain National Park. Dogs are not permitted in the park and other, somewhat more stringent, regulations are enforced. Be aware of these.

GETTING THERE: From Allenspark, drive north on Colorado 7 about 8.4 miles and turn right, onto the Forest Service road at the Lily Lake Visitor Center. From Estes Park, drive south on Colorado 7 about 6.3 miles and turn left onto the Forest Service road at the Lily Lake Visitor Center. Park at the Visitor Center or drive up the road about 0.4 mile and park in the designated area.

THE ROUTE: The trail begins at the turnaround and barrier on this Forest Service road; start measuring distances from here. Hike up the road about 500 feet to the kiosk. From the kiosk go left (east) to the first switchback, at 0.2 mile. After the third switchback, at 0.5 mile, you will be heading south. At 1.2 miles, an overlook to your right allows great views of the valley below and of Longs Peak rising up out of the valley.

Proceed past this overlook, along a cliff to your left, to the fourth switchback, at 1.4 miles. Here the trail joins the older, more-established

Mount Meeker and Longs Peak across the valley from the Twin Sisters Trail.   PHOTO BY ART ROBERTS

section of the trail and continues to climb and switch back as you quickly gain altitude. As you climb higher, the views of Longs Peak become more impressive. At mile 2.9, look to the northwest to view the Mummy Range. See if you can pick out the Y on the face of Mount Ypsilon. At mile 3.2, leave the tree cover behind as you look up to the summit. Look for the radio tower that marks the top and the first of the two peaks. You can easily spot Lake Estes and the city of Estes Park in the valley below to the north.

When you reach the saddle between the two Twin Sisters peaks, the first summit is on your right and the second is to the left. From this saddle, you will see Twin Sisters Mountain to the southeast. Turn to your right and head up the easy trail to the first summit, just past the research building. This summit gives shelter from strong winds and offers great views. The Mummy Range is to the northwest, Longs Peak is to the west, and the Indian Peaks Wilderness to the southwest.

After reaching the first peak, consider going over to the second peak to the east. Look for cairns marking a moderate scramble and climb to the top. This summit is a bit harder than the easy summit by the radio tower. The elevation here is 11,428 feet.

Getting to Twin Sisters Mountain is quite a bit more difficult than getting to Twin Sisters Peaks. Don't attempt this if you don't have good footwear and are not skilled in difficult, steep, and strenuous rock scrambles. If you do go, be sure to minimize your impact to this fragile environment.

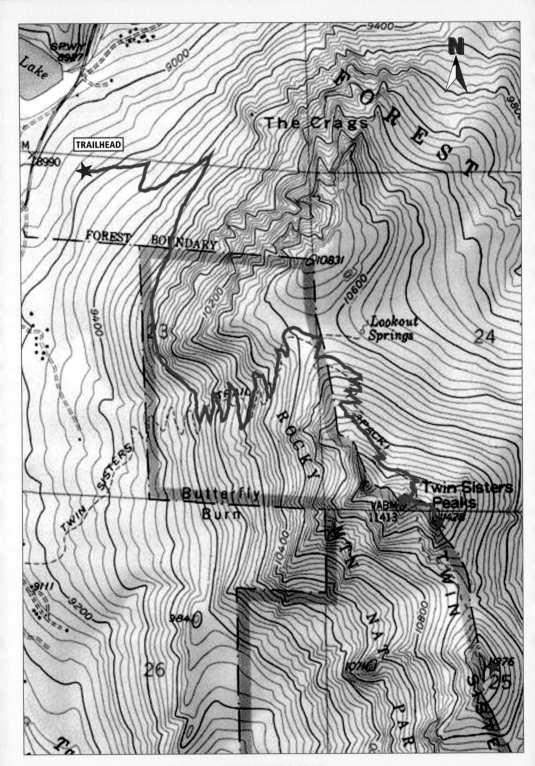

TWIN SISTERS PEAK

37. Walker Ranch Loop

BY FRANÇOISE COOPERMAN

MAPS	Trails Illustrated, Boulder/Golden, Number 100 USGS, Eldorado Springs, 7.5 minute CMC Trail Map, Boulder Mountain Parks and Nearby Open Space
ELEVATION GAIN	890 feet
RATING	Moderate
ROUND-TRIP DISTANCE	7.6 miles
ROUND-TRIP TIME	5–7 hours
NEAREST LANDMARK	Boulder

COMMENT: This long loop offers a wide variety of scenery, ranging from riverbanks to expansive valley overlooks. The hike is neither technical nor extreme, but it does provide a great workout. A brochure at the trailhead contains a map, the history of this large cattle ranch from the 1800s, and information on the local flora, fauna, and geology. The trail is clearly signed and has prominent mile markers and other informative signs along the entire loop. The multiuse trail can be quite crowded on weekends. Dogs are allowed, but leash laws are strictly enforced.

GETTING THERE: In Boulder, take Baseline Road toward the mountains. As it begins to climb, it turns into Flagstaff Road. Follow it for about 8 miles. The South Boulder Creek Trailhead (Walker Ranch Loop Trailhead) is clearly marked on the left, at a sharp bend in the road. A short dirt road leads to the parking lot.

THE ROUTE: The trail can be done in either direction, but starting by going right follows the mile markers (MMs in this description) and makes some of the difficult stretches easier. The trail begins as an old road, with a long, gradual descent through rock formations, and an old burn area from a six-day fire in 2000. There is not much shade, so hot days can be taxing.

The path gradually gets steeper, eventually reaching a brook crossing, complete with flittering butterflies and lush foliage. A charming picnic area is near MM 1, alongside the quickly flowing South Boulder Creek. An easy path continues along the river into a rocky canyon. Look for birds, snakes, lizards, and various rodents. Fly-fishing is popular near the bridge. Turn left at the signpost.

The Crescent Meadows branch of the Walker Ranch Loop.

For a side trip, go straight along a charming path next to the river's edge. It dead-ends after 0.25 mile, at private property. From the signpost, begin a long, steady climb on a wide path. Beware of loose gravel and speedy cyclists. MM 2 marks the end of the hill. The trail flattens out for a bit, enters Eldorado Canyon State Park, passes through dappled forest, and then slopes up again to a series of switchbacks that end at Crescent Meadows parking lot. There is a view of Gross Dam and the occasional train passing on the nearby tracks.

An easy trail continues through hilly, open grasslands. Patches of colorful wildflowers dot the fields. Exit the meadow at MM 3 and begin wrapping around the hillside. Between the trees are picturesque views of Eldorado Canyon. The forest thickens as the path descends, with some switchbacks. Rule signs mark the re-entrance into Boulder County Parks and Open Space.

MM 4 finds the trail still wrapping downward. It briefly splits into two routes, based on the technical skill of cyclists. Both are enjoyable, but expect some rocks on the lower trail. The roar of water can be heard as the trail reaches the cliff edge. While perhaps not for very cautious hikers, the steep, exposed trail down is well built, with deep log stairs and strategic rocks. Rushing cascades wait at the bottom, and many people rest at the small waterfall here.

After a bridge, the trail leads away from the creek and comes to a sign marking the Eldorado Canyon Trail, one of the other trails described in this book. The trail continues as an old road, heading up steeply at MM 5. Watch for loose dirt in this part. The pathway slopes its way up and down to the remains of an old homestead. Turn left at a junction. (Straight will take you to another trailhead and picnic area.) The trail returns to the forest by MM 6 and then meanders along the bottom of a rocky outcropping. Leaving the lush vegetation, you head up into a dark fir and pine forest. After a long climb and a few switchbacks, you will emerge on the top of the ridge, and be rewarded with lovely views. A pleasant stroll continues along the undulating hillside. After MM 7, charred trees mark the landscape as the trail returns to the parking lot.

South Boulder Creek, near the bottom of the steep descent from the Crescent Meadows Trail.

PHOTO BY FRANÇOISE COOPERMAN

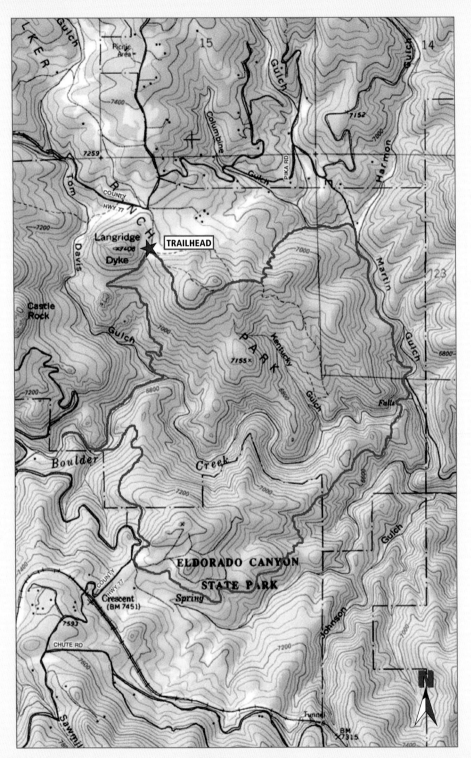

WALKER RANCH LOOP

38. Barr Trail to Pikes Peak (14,115 feet)

BY KEVIN BAKER

MAPS	Trails Illustrated, Pikes Peak/Cañon City, Number 137
ELEVATION GAIN	7,400 feet
RATING	Difficult
ROUND-TRIP DISTANCE	25.8 miles
ROUND-TRIP TIME	9–14 hours
NEAREST LANDMARK	Manitou Springs

COMMENT: Pikes Peak marks the end of the prairie and the beginning of Colorado's vast Rocky Mountains. It was first climbed in 1820 and has since seen millions of visitors, most by way of either the cog railway or the Pikes Peak Highway. Ironically, Zebulon Pike, for whom the peak is named, never made it to the summit. Katherine Lee Bates was inspired to write "America the Beautiful" atop the mountain, earning Pikes the nickname "America's Mountain." Although not at all technically challenging, a trek up Barr Trail to the summit of Pikes is a worthy accomplishment.

Pikes via Barr Trail has the most vertical gain of any 14er in Colorado. A dayhike of Pikes is a huge day, so most folks split up the hike into at least two days, with a stay at Barr Camp, some 6.5 miles up the trail, at 10,200 feet. Barr Camp offers many accommodations, including a main bunkhouse, a private cabin, lean-to shelters, and tent sites. Breakfast and dinner are available by reservation, and hot and cold drinks are sold all day. This historic place sees over 20,000 visitors per year, with most coming in the summer. Visit www.barrcamp.com for information on rates or to make reservations.

GETTING THERE: From U.S. 24, take the Manitou Springs exit and turn west onto Manitou Avenue. Continue 1.4 miles west to Ruxton Avenue. Turn left on Ruxton and continue up this narrow road 1.0 mile to Hydro Street, just beyond the parking area for the cog railway. Go right on Hydro and up the steep, narrow street to the trailhead. Parking may be difficult. On weekends, you may have to park below the cog railway on Ruxton.

THE ROUTE: Barr Trail has a variety of terrain that will challenge every peakbagger. The first 3.0 miles of trail will test you with a series of switch-backs up the steep southeast slopes. After passing under a natural rock arch,

The trail near Lightning Point.   PHOTO BY PAUL DOYLE

the trail zigs its way steeply up the south slopes, then gradually heads west, contouring along the south slopes of Rocky Mountain. Continue west at the trail junction with a spur trail that leads to the top of the incline.

After 3.2 miles, a sign at No Name Creek advises Barr Camp is only 3.5 miles away. Most of the vertical to Barr Camp is done and the rest of the way is much easier. Be aware that every trail sign indicating mileage will be utterly wrong. Head left at the sign, following the creek for a bit. Be sure to stay right at the junction with the unsigned Pipeline Trail. Miss and you can end up in Ruxton Park!

After a few more steep switchbacks, the terrain mellows out and there are flat sections to recuperate on. Some of the best views of Pikes can be obtained by scrambling just off the trail. Lightning Point is a rock outcropping just a few yards off the trail to the south, beyond the 7.8 miles to summit sign. Monte's View Rockpile is a fun scramble just 1.0 mile from Barr Camp south of the trail, although you'll have to do some rough bushwhacking to get up it!

The section from No Name Creek offers some nice downhill options for a change of pace. After a few steeper sections, you finally arrive at Barr Camp. Barr is a good place to refuel and fill up your water if you're dayhiking, although the water is untreated and requires purification. Barr Camp has Gatorade, bottled water, and snacks.

The second half of the hike to the summit is much tougher, due to the thinning air, but the many switchbacks keep the overall steepness of the trail manageable. I like to break this journey into segments: the first is Barr Camp to the Bottomless Pit Trail. A series of long switchbacks leads up the forest, with beautiful bristlecone pine trees along the way. The trail is quite a bit rockier above Barr Camp, but wide and easy to follow. After 1.0 mile, there is a sign for the Bottomless Pit, an enchanting place below the north face of Pikes that few people get a chance to visit. Bottomless Pit is at the base of the Y and Railroad couloirs, a couple of fun, moderate snow climbs for experienced mountaineers using technical climbing gear. Be sure to take the switchback left at this trail junction.

The trail then zigs and zags its way up to A-Frame, a shelter that some opt to camp at, near treeline at 12,000 feet. I find this section of the hike to be the longest. In winter, with decent snow conditions, a viable option from treeline is to follow a prominent low-angle gully of snow all the way up to the summit. Other times, follow short switchbacks to around 12,800 feet, at the base of where the east ridge steepens. The trail then does a long traverse across the broad east face, gently climbing 400 feet to a view down into a dramatic bowl known as the Cirque. Enjoy what is probably the most dramatic spot along the trail.

After a few short switchbacks along the edge of the Cirque, there is a sign announcing one mile to the summit. The trail zigs its way up the upper east face, with a few shorter traverses, until the infamous 16 Golden Stairs, a reference to the number of switchbacks left on the trail—there are actually 32 of them. The trail now gets rockier and requires clambering over boulders, but keep pressing on and you'll soon pop out at the end of the train tracks. The summit is not your typical 14er, as you will likely be sharing it with tourists who have either ridden the cog railway or driven up the Pikes Peak Highway.

It is sometimes possible to either ride the train or hitch a ride down, but don't count on it happening. Be prepared to make the long slog all the way back to the bottom. Make certain to visit the true summit of Pikes, amid an indistinct jumble of boulders in the middle of the parking lot. Doughnuts and pizza are available at the summit house, a rare treat on a 14er. Barr Trail is a classic that anyone in decent shape can experience—give it a shot.

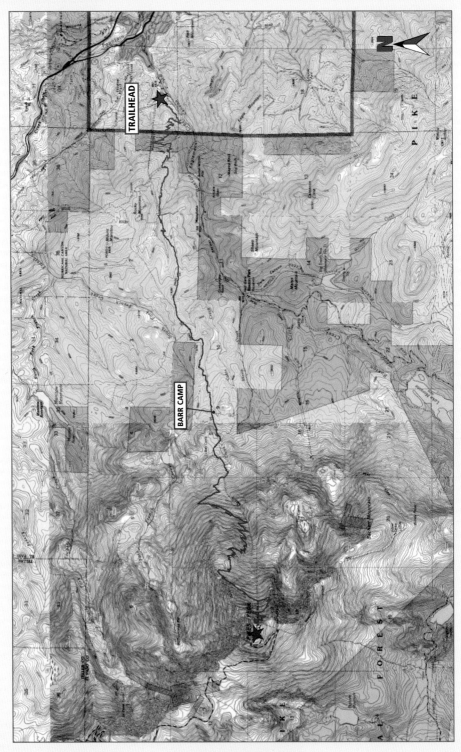

BARR TRAIL TO PIKES PEAK

39. Catamount Trail

BY DR. TRAJN BOUGHAN

MAPS	Trails Illustrated, Pikes Peak/Cañon City, Number 137
ELEVATION GAIN	1,400 feet
RATING	Easy–moderate
ROUND-TRIP DISTANCE	5.5 miles
ROUND-TRIP TIME	2–4 hours
NEAREST LANDMARK	Green Mountain Falls

COMMENT: The town of Green Mountain Falls hosts a city park on a mountain slope—the Catamount Trail. The trail scales a sidewall of the Ute Pass, a slot canyon rising from Manitou Springs into the Rocky Mountains. Catamount Creek, and nearby Crystal Creek, fall from the canyon's edge. Catamount is another name for a Colorado mountain lion.

The Catamount Trail is an out-and-back trip between Green Mountain Falls and the North and South Catamount and Crystal Creek reservoirs. Start early enough to return before summer thunderstorms. The trail is well maintained and easy to follow, with little blue dots nailed to the trees.

GETTING THERE: Take U.S. 24 west from Colorado Springs. From the traffic light at Cascade, drive about 4 miles and take the second exit marked Green Mountain Falls, Chipita Park. The ramp drops into the commercial district; park on the main street, Ute Pass Avenue.

THE ROUTE: The hike's staging area is downtown, with two ways to reach the wilderness trailhead. The northern approach, by Belvedere Avenue, ascends gradually. The more direct, more demanding, southerly route climbs straight up to the top of Hondo Avenue. The Catamount Trail officially begins at the waterworks' road bridge on Hondo Avenue.

The zigzag route gains elevation quickly and keeps returning to the creek-side, allowing water play at tiny beaches. Many hikers are content to reach the waterfall, where the color-coded trail markers diverge. An informal tied-log footbridge, topped by teetering flat stones, allows a stream crossing to join the yellow-dot Thomas Trail. This connects back to the upper reaches of Boulder Street in town.

The Catamount's diversionary trail veers away from the creek and takes a long northerly traverse, headed toward a saddle in the ridge above. A narrow single-track skirts the base of the Dome Rock outcropping. An optional short

Living the good life.

spur steps up to a rocky promontory overlooking the town. Look across the valley to see how far the opposite Rampart Range ridgeline keeps dropping while your own climb gains altitude.

Near the crest, a forest of blue dots guides you across sheer rock whose thin soils cannot hold a constructed trail bed. The hard climb is finally over once you've reached the cross-path. Long-distance views open down both sides of the knife-edge ridge. Turquoise-dot signs point out another spur for a panoramic view over Ute Pass.

The main trail of the plain blue dots drops from the ridge, going straight down into a fanciful place called the Garden of Eden. The packed-dirt path moves into a sunny meadow. The south slope, covered in spruce, fir, and ponderosa pine, is confronted across the valley floor by a high, wavy wall of granular granite, wind-whipped to form hoodoo columns. Catamount Creek reappears as an innocent meander through a marsh, with broadleaf vegetation, shadowed groves, juvenile blue spruce succeeding aspens after a fire, and seasonal wildflowers.

Ambitious hikers can walk farther, after crossing the low creek on a log, to find the South Catamount Reservoir. Engineered scenery disrupts the natural ambience beyond the gate, where a dusty service road passes underneath the reservoir's massive rubble wall. Red raspberries ripen by the roadside at the end of August, sweetening the outlook. A view of Pikes Peak greets your arrival at the top of the dam. Families drive in from the Pikes Peak Toll Road to picnic and motorboat. Look down to see anglers settled in chairs portaged from the parking lot. Be sure to return to the gate by 4 p.m., when the reservoir park closes for the day.

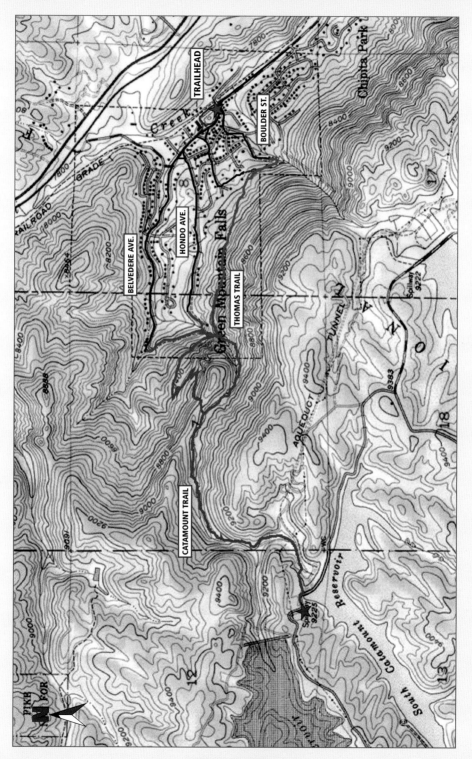

CATAMOUNT TRAIL

40. Lizard Rock – Lake Park Loop

BY GREG LONG

MAPS	Trails Illustrated, Tarryall Mountains/Kenosha Pass, Number 105
ELEVATION GAIN	Lizard Rock: 1,000 feet; full loop: 3,600 feet
RATING	Lizard Rock: easy–moderate; full loop: moderate–difficult
ROUND-TRIP DISTANCE	Lizard Rock: 5 miles; full loop: 15.1 miles
ROUND-TRIP TIME	Lizard Rock: 2–3 hours; full loop: 7–10 hours
NEAREST LANDMARK	Lake George

COMMENT: Most of this loop lies within the Lost Creek Wilderness, a pristine area found—incredibly—within an hour's drive of both Colorado Springs and Denver. Be it summer wildflowers, fall's colors, unique granite formations, or just a quiet space for meditation and reflection, Lost Creek provides it.

The Lizard Rock Trail provides a short outing over mild terrain to its namesake rock formation and great views of the wilderness and, all the way west, the Sawatch Range. Continuing the loop over Hankins Pass to Lake Park provides an intense all-day workout or delightful weekend backpack. The trail is well maintained with good signage throughout.

The Lost Creek Wilderness has many interconnecting trails, allowing for excellent multiday backpacking opportunities, of which this loop is just one.

GETTING THERE: Take U.S. 24 west from Colorado Springs for 37 miles to Lake George and turn right onto County Road 77. Travel 12.8 miles and turn right, into Spruce Grove Campground. Dayhikers should park outside the fence; the trail leaves from inside the campground, behind the pit toilets.

THE ROUTE: Cross the bridge over the creek and take an immediate left onto Lizard Rock Trail #658. Pass through a short rock tunnel and stay on the main track, over gentle ups and downs and through open meadows with views of the rock formations above. Switchbacks and a steeper grade begin after 2.0 miles; at 2.3. miles, take the right fork for the loop toward Lake Park, or take a hard left for the side trail to Lizard Rock. To get to the Rock, scramble steeply for 0.25 mile and enjoy great 360-degree views of the Lost Creek Wilderness.

To continue on the loop, pass the Wilderness sign and, at 2.4 miles, take another right fork. Trail #658 becomes Trail #630. Look for a sign indicating To Lake Park/Goose Creek Campground (the sign is not visible until after the turn) and follow up well-graded switchbacks to Hankins Pass, at 3.9 miles.

Lake Park.

At the pass, turn left (west) on Lake Park Trail #639. The trail climbs steeply along a ridge toward Lake Park. Pause to scramble up one of the many rock formations and take in the views. Look back to the southeast to see the burn scar from the 2002 Hayman Fire, which started in this area and burned over 138,000 acres. At 5.7 miles, descend into Lake Park, an open area with wild-flowers, rock formations, and excellent fall colors. Level camping spots are plentiful and water is available at the west end of the park.

After many ups and downs, the trail finally tops out at 7.4 miles, at 11,580 feet. Begin descending on steep, loose trail before the angle lessens in a lush coniferous forest. At 8.6 miles, watch for a sign indicating the Brookside Trail #607. Turn left (south) and follow the Brookside Trail for 2 miles, where it connects back with Trail #658. There are additional good camping spots along here. Turn left (southeast) at the Spruce Grove C.G. 3, Hankins Pass 3 sign and climb back to the saddle with the Lizard Rock turnoff. Follow Trail #658 back to the parking area.

SIDEBAR: McCURDY MOUNTAIN

The Lake Park loop can be connected with the McCurdy Mountain Trail, on page 154 in this guide. At 8.6 miles in the directions above, turn north instead of south on Trail #607 to reach McCurdy Mountain. This could make a scenic additional day on a backpack trip or a challenging side trip for a dayhiking masochist.

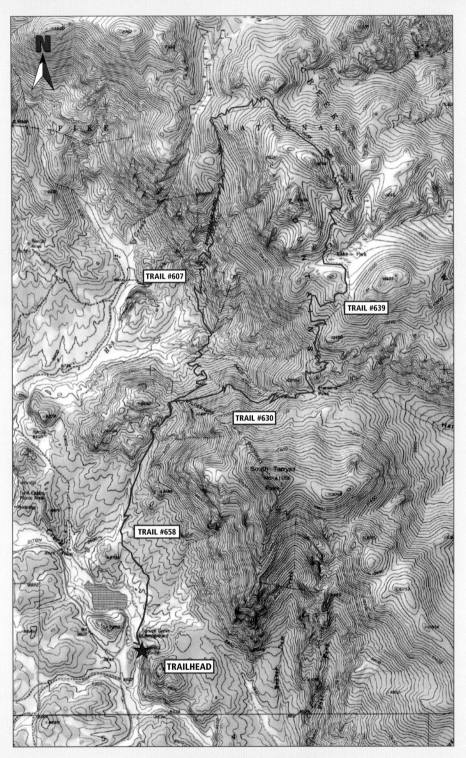

TRAIL #607

TRAIL #639

TRAIL #630

TRAIL #658

TRAILHEAD

LIZARD ROCK – LAKE PARK LOOP

41. Lovell Gulch

BY ALEX PAUL

MAPS	Trails Illustrated, Pikes Peak/Cañon City, Number 137
ELEVATION GAIN	1,000 feet
RATING	Easy–moderate
ROUND-TRIP DISTANCE	5.5 miles
ROUND-TRIP TIME	3 hours
NEAREST LANDMARK	Woodland Park

COMMENT: Lovell Gulch is a pleasant loop trail winding through the sub-alpine ponderosa/spruce forest of the Rocky Mountain foothills. The gulch offers views of open ponderosa pine and grassy meadows on south-facing slopes and thick spruce forest covering the north-facing slopes. The meadows and forest display a wide variety of wildflowers throughout the growing season, from wild iris and lady slippers in early summer to thistle and mariposa lily later in summer, and a myriad of flowers that bloom throughout the summer. The secluded valleys are habitat for mule deer, elk, bear, fox, and coyote. Wildlife is commonly observed from the trail early in the morning or near dusk.

Outlooks from the highpoint of the loop trail afford panoramic views of Wilkerson Pass, Crystal Peak, the Tarryall Mountains, the Hayman Fire burn area, and, on clear days, the snowcapped peaks of the Sawatch Range far to the west. Descending the ridge on the back side of the loop allows glimpses of Pikes Peak through the trees to the south.

Lovell Gulch is also a popular trail with equestrians and mountain bikers. Dogs are allowed, but keep them under control in order not to disturb wildlife and other trail users.

GETTING THERE: From the U.S. 24/Cimarron exit, number 141, on Interstate 25, take U.S. 24 west 17.2 miles to Woodland Park. At the third stoplight in Woodland Park, in view of the City of Woodland Park sign, turn right onto Baldwin Street. Proceed 2.1 miles, passing the high school campus, where Baldwin Street becomes Rampart Range Road, to the City of Woodland Park maintenance shop on the left. Pull off and park along the fence south of the shop. The trailhead is visible to the west. Proceed through the gate in the fence to access the trail.

THE ROUTE: The Lovell Gulch Trail is generally well defined and consists of

Pikes Peak north face.

a wide single-track or narrower double-track paths. It is well graded with fine granite gravel covering the tread, with only scattered washouts.

From the gate, follow the trail for about 0.5 mile along the edge of the city shop and some residences. Continue on through the forest to a trail intersection at 0.8 mile. Take the left fork down and across the creek. (Save the right fork for some future variation.) Across the creek, a sign marks the start of the Lovell Gulch Loop Trail (3¾ miles). Take the right fork and hike the trail counterclockwise. The trail follows the creek along the bottom of Lovell Gulch, with ponderosa pine on the left slope and heavy spruce on the right. As the trail ascends the gulch, the valley narrows, with large granite boulders on the slopes close to the trail.

At 2.4 miles, the trail tops at Rampart Range Road. Walk left through the vehicle barricade and follow under the power line to the west. At 3.3 miles, the trail crosses under the power line and veers northwest away from it. The trail then climbs a knoll, with grand views of Pikes Peak, Woodland Park, and the mountains to the west. From this knoll, the trail drops steeply to the west until it turns south and follows along the boundary fence between national forest and privately owned land, back to the Lovell Gulch Loop sign. Bear right and follow the previously taken access trail back to the parking lot.

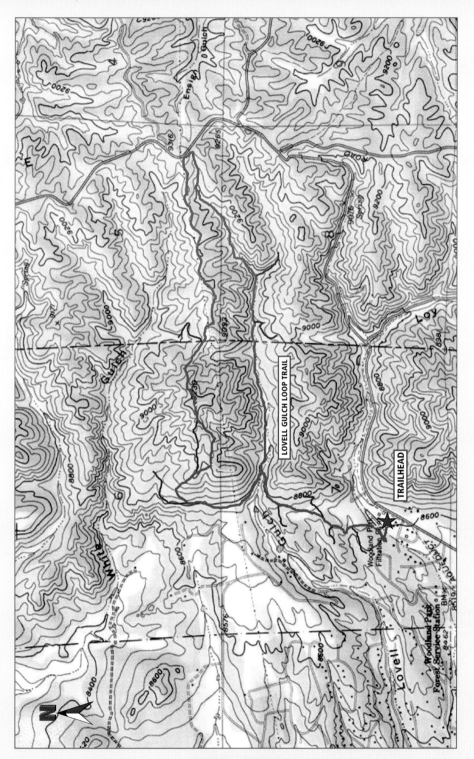

LOVELL GULCH

42. McCurdy Mountain

BY ERIC SWAB

MAPS	Trails Illustrated, Tarryall Mountains/Kenosha Pass, Number 105 USGS, McCurdy Mountain, 7.5 minute
ELEVATION GAIN	4,270 feet
RATING	Difficult
ROUND-TRIP DISTANCE	17.25 miles
ROUND-TRIP TIME	8–10 hours
NEAREST LANDMARK	Twin Eagles Campground on County Road 77

COMMENT: McCurdy Mountain's 12,168-foot summit is the second highest in the Tarryall Mountains, part of the Lost Creek Wilderness. Lost Creek is renowned for its incredible red granite rock formations. Unlike many of the Rocky Mountains' broken crags, these are soft and convoluted, forming fanciful shapes.

The destination campground is a Pike National Forest fee area, and parking for the day is $3.00, or $1.50 with a Golden Age Passport. Registration for entry into the wilderness is free. It helps the Forest Service track use of the area and provides the hiker with information about its protection.

There is a pit toilet south of the main parking area. Dogs on a leash and horses are permitted on the trail. Bicycles are not allowed in the wilderness.

In summer, carry three to four liters of water, less if you have a filter or tablets. A compass will help with off-trail route finding near the summit, especially if clouds move in and obscure the landmarks.

GETTING THERE: From Colorado Springs, take U.S. 24 west; 1.0 mile west of the town of Lake George, turn right at the sign to Tarryall. Follow Park County Road 77 for 17 miles to the Twin Eagles Campground, at 8,550 feet.

THE ROUTE: The trailhead is at the north end of the campground parking lot. From the trailhead, cross a bridge over Tarryall Creek and turn left. The wilderness registration box is at 0.4 mile. Turn left onto the old wagon road, Forest Service Trail #607. A sign at 2.1 miles says Twin Eagles TH 2, pointing back the way you came, and McCurdy Park 4, pointing in the direction you want. The side trail sign says Spruce Grove C.G. 3, Hankins Pass 3.

Climbing gets serious at 2.75 miles. At 3.0 miles, watch for Lizard Rock, a large formation perched on top of a treed knob, across the valley to the

Granite spires.

southwest. At 3.25 miles, enter the Lost Creek Wilderness Area. Watch for a rock window on your left, with a rock needle sticking up in the middle, around 4.25 miles. At 5.2 miles, reach a saddle and another junction signed Lake Park Tr No. 639 to the right and Brookside Trail No. 607, your route, straight ahead. The trail descends here to a stream crossing and your last chance to refill your water containers.

As you climb out of this drainage, you will come to another junction. The sign announces McCurdy Park Tr. No. 628, straight ahead, and Brookside Tr. No. 607, to the left. Stay on 607. At 6.8 miles, enter the realm of the silver-gray ghosts of a forest fire that predated 1898. These weathered snags, set against the backdrop of red granite ramparts, compose some of the finest natural sculpture in Colorado.

At 7.0 miles you will begin to see young limber and bristlecone pine growing, probably the descendants of the burned trees. From here, cross three minor ridges. At the third ridge, mile 8, you will leave the trail. There is no sign. Please do not follow in someone else's footsteps—this will lessen your impact on the fragile alpine tundra.

Begin your off-trail excursion on compass heading 30°, toward the lowest point on the horizon. Passing above the long, low ridge of layered granite, you will be in a broad valley between two rocky ridges. Stay low in the valley until you are near the saddle. This will allow you to judge which rock outcropping is the highest. The outcroppings to the right and left are both McCurdy. The one to the southeast (right) is 4 feet higher and is the actual summit. The easiest scramble to the top is from the northeast, to the climber's left. There are just a few moves for which you will need to use your hands.

From the summit, you have a 360-degree view of the world. At 10° is Windy Peak (11,970 feet) and at 50° is Buffalo Peak (11,589 feet), both in the Lost Creek Wilderness. At 100° is the 2002 Hayman Fire area; at 115° is Pikes Peak (14,115 feet); at 250° is the Sawatch Range; and at 330°, Bison Peak (12,431 feet). Return the way you came.

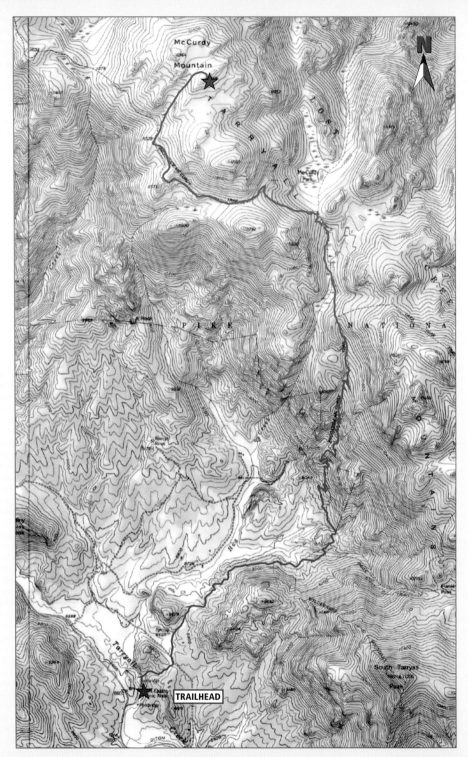

McCURDY MOUNTAIN

43. Mount Herman

BY KATE STEWART

MAPS	Trails Illustrated, Pikes Peak/Cañon City, Number 137
ELEVATION GAIN	1,000 feet
RATING	Easy–moderate
ROUND-TRIP DISTANCE	2.1 miles
ROUND-TRIP TIME	1–2 hours
NEAREST LANDMARK	Town of Monument/Pikes Peak Hot Shots Fire Center

COMMENT: Forest Service Trail #716 offers a quiet, usually secluded hike. The path is steep, rough, and eroded. It can be treacherous on a rainy day. Mount Herman has been climbed for years. A CMC hike was reported on this trail in 1913. It is still beautiful and wild.

GETTING THERE: From Colorado Springs, take Interstate 25 north to the Monument exit (exit 161). Turn left at the light at the end of the exit ramp onto Highway 105. Follow this road back across I-25 and go straight through the lights, onto Second Street.

Follow Second Street across a set of railroad tracks to a stop sign at Mitchell Avenue. (It is approximately 1.0 mile from the exit ramp to this stop sign.) Turn left and follow Mitchell Avenue for 0.6 mile. Turn right onto Mount Herman Road. In 1.5 miles, this road turns from pavement to dirt. The trailhead is 3.3 miles from where the pavement ends and the dirt begins.

Note that there is a Mount Herman trailhead at the corner of Nursery Road and Mount Herman Road. Don't get confused: your trailhead is several miles farther. Mount Herman Road is a four-wheel-drive road. It is rutted and challenging, but manageable in passenger cars. Use extra caution if the weather is rainy.

The trailhead is at a tight left turn in the road. It will be on the right and has space for about seven cars. There are no signs at the trailhead, so rely on your odometer.

A trail marker, Forest Service Trail #716, is on the right of the trail as you begin your hike.

THE ROUTE: The well-used trail follows a small mountain stream on your left. Watch for false trails that lead off from the main trail.

You will pass through a flower-filled meadow. We identified purple asters, black-eyed Susans, purple bee balm, large bluebells, and tiny blue harebells.

Air Force Academy Chapel in the distance.

This hike is not very long, but it makes up for the distance by the aggressive uphill climb of 1,000 feet in just over a mile.

The path follows the stream until it turns to the right and goes up a hill. At this fork, a faint, dead-end trail leads off to the left.

Instead, follow the trail to the right and up the hill until it switchbacks to the left and leads upwards through the trees. The trail is eroded and water runoff is apparent. At this turn, there is another trail leading off to the right to a nice overlook.

After 0.75 mile, the trail turns to the right and continues steeply through rockfall. Cairns lead the way through the rocks. Once up the rockfall, a meadow leads to a steep drop-off to the valley below. There is a long summit ridge; the highpoint is at the furthest left (north) side of the ridge. From here, there are lovely views of Monument and its surrounding lakes, the Air Force Academy, and Pikes Peak to the south. On a clear day, you may see Mt. Evans and Longs Peak to the north.

Spend some time at the top. There is plenty of shade and there are plenty of photo opportunities. It is a great place for a picnic if you want.

You return on the same trail, and now the words are: steep downhill, watch your footing. Regardless of the ups and the downs of the trail, the views make it all worthwhile. Enjoy.

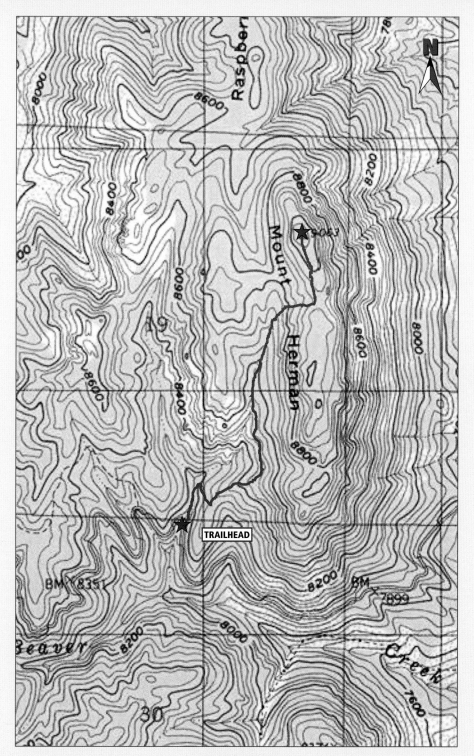

MOUNT HERMAN

44. Mueller State Park – Cheesman Ranch and Outlook Ridge Geer Pond Loop

BY STUART HISER

MAPS	Trails Illustrated, Pikes Peak/Cañon City, Number 137 Visitor's Center trail map
ELEVATION GAIN	Cheesman: 1,200 feet; Outlook: 800 feet
RATING	Cheesman: moderate; Outlook: easy
ROUND-TRIP DISTANCE	Cheesman: 8–8.5 miles; Outlook: 4–4.5 miles
ROUND-TRIP TIME	Cheesman: 4–5 hours; Outlook: 1.5–2 hours
NEAREST LANDMARK	Divide

COMMENT: Mueller State Park provides over 50 miles of varied hiking trails within 45 minutes of town. The Cheesman Ranch hike includes the Cheesman Ranch homestead. Although closed, most buildings are largely intact. There are views of the west side of Pikes Peak, and herds of elk are not uncommon. In the fall, the aspen groves are in full color. The ranch offers many shady spots for a picnic lunch, while the easy Outlook Ridge Geer Pond Loop hike introduces you to the trails at Mueller. This part of the park is closed in late spring for elk calving.

There is a park entrance fee per vehicle per visit.

GETTING THERE: From Colorado Springs, take U.S. 24 west to Divide. Turn left (south) on Colorado 67 and continue 5.0 miles to the park entrance. Follow the main road through the park, into the campground, to the Peak View Trailhead. There is water and a restroom at this trailhead.

THE ROUTE:

CHEESMAN RANCH: Begin east on Trail #19, Peak View. Pass Peak View Pond on your right (a spur trail leads down to the pond). At the junction with Trail #18, Elk Meadow, turn left (north). Where this trail joins with Trail #17, Cheesman Ranch, continue straight ahead (north). The trail passes Rule Creek Pond as it makes its way northward through an open meadow. At the far north end of the park, the trail bears west as it passes the Cheesman Ranch homestead. Past the homestead, the trail turns back to the south and starts a long climb uphill into the trees. To your right, you will pass Trail #32,

Sentinel Point.

Dynamite Cabin—an optional 1.0 mile side loop that rejoins Trail #17.

Not far from the campground, the trail comes to a three-way junction. Here you could take Trail #16 to the top of Grouse Mountain overlook, about a 0.5-mile out-and-back, for some nice views and a good place to stop for lunch.

From the three-way junction, Trail #17 continues east. At the junction with Trail #35 (Lost Still), there is another optional side loop to Cahil Pond: turn left on Trail #35, right on Trail #34 (Cahil Pond), right on Trail #36 (Moonshine), and finally rejoin Trail #17 to your left. Where the trail rejoins Trail #18, turn right (south). Continue to the junction with Trail #19, and turn right (west). This will return to your starting point.

For a longer hike, you can begin at the Elk Meadow Trailhead. Begin east on Trail #18 (Elk Meadow), and then follow the same route as above.

OUTLOOK RIDGE: Follow the main road through the park, just past the Visitor Center, to the Outlook Ridge picnic area and trailhead. You will find water and a restroom at this trailhead. Trail #7 (Outlook Ridge) begins to the west from the picnic area. After 0.5 mile, you will pass three side trails: #8, #9, and #10, which all lead to overlook points. Each is a 0.5-mile out-and-back, and affords good views of the park.

Trail #7 ends at the junction with Trail #25 (Geer Pond); turn left (west). After 0.25 mile, pass Geer Pond on your left (note that this part of the trail can be muddy). Bear right (north) onto Trail #26 (Beaver Ponds), continue to the junction with Trail #12 (Homestead), and turn right. As you near the Homestead Trailhead, you will find Trail #1 (Revenuer's Ridge) to your right. This goes through the Lost Pond picnic area, then rejoins Trail #7. Turn left and return to the starting point.

Many other hikes are possible from here; Mueller is worth returning to over and over again—consult the trail map, available from the Visitor Center, for details.

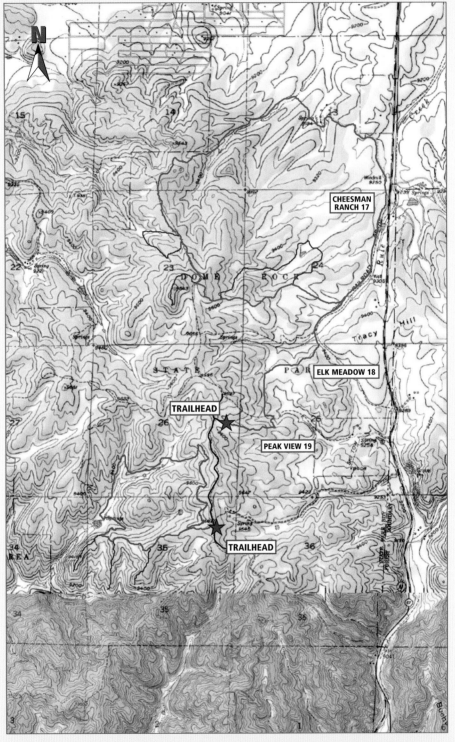

MUELLER STATE PARK – CHEESMAN RANCH AND OUTLOOK RIDGE GEER POND LOOP

45. Palmer Lake Reservoirs and Cap Rock

BY BOB HOSTETLER

MAPS	Trails Illustrated, Pikes Peak/Cañon City, Number 137 USGS, Mt. Deception, 7.5 minute
ELEVATION GAIN	To second reservoir: 600 feet; to top of loop: 840 feet; to Cap Rock: 1,330 feet
RATING	Easy to scrambling/difficult
ROUND-TRIP DISTANCE	To second reservoir: 2.4 miles; for Ice Cave loop: 3.7 miles; for Cap Rock: 5.0 miles
ROUND-TRIP TIME	1–5 hours
NEAREST LANDMARK	Palmer Lake Town Hall

COMMENT: The two Palmer Lake Reservoirs and the area trails have a rich history dating to the last decades of the nineteenth century. The road to the reservoirs—built in 1887 and 1903—is occasionally used by maintenance vehicles and provides a steep, invigorating start to area hikes. Visiting the reservoirs alone provides excellent views in a peaceful valley and water setting. Heading out on one of the unimproved trails can feel like being in a very remote spot only a mile from the trailhead. Hikers who enjoy scrambling can reach a spectacular summit, the size of a dining room table, 250 feet above the ground on three sides. The early history of hiking in the area includes the second official hike by the CMC. This was on June 20, 1912, when Lucretia Vaile, an early Palmer Lake resident, led a group up the Reservoir Road, Balanced Rock Road, and Rampart Range Road to Woodland Park.

GETTING THERE: Take Interstate 25 to the Monument/Palmer Lake exit #161. Turn left onto Colorado 105 and follow it when it turns right after crossing I-25. Follow 105 for 3.8 miles and watch for a Speed Limit 30 sign on the right and turn left onto South Valley Road (the road sign is not visible until after you've made the turn). Drive west on South Valley Road 0.4 mile and turn left on Old Carriage Road. Park at the bottom of the hill.

THE ROUTES:

PALMER LAKE RESERVOIRS: Hike west on the trail for 200 yards, until it joins the reservoir access road (FS 322). Hike up this steep road for 0.6 mile

Upper reservoir.

to the first reservoir. Continue for 0.6 mile more to the second and much larger reservoir, a great spot for picnicking or fishing.

RESERVOIR/ICE CAVE CREEK LOOP: Follow the above route to the lower reservoir. At the upper end of the lower reservoir, the road takes a hard left and turns uphill. At this point (yellow trail on map), turn right, onto a rough, unimproved trail along the left side of Ice Cave Creek and its boulder field. (Ice Cave Creek is so-named because "caves" formed under the huge rocks in this canyon hold ice well into the summer. Be very careful attempting to explore these caves.) At 1.2 miles from the trailhead, cross the creek. At 1.4 miles, you will T into a north/south trail that shows evidence of having been a two-track, four-wheel-drive road in years past. Turn south and follow this trail for 1.0 mile, back across Ice Cave Creek, up and over a ridge, then steeply down to an arm of the second reservoir, at 2.4 miles. Turn left to return to the trailhead.

CAP ROCK (a.k.a. ROCK DOME): An attempt on this rocky peak should be undertaken only by those comfortable with scrambling and some exposure. No technical climbing skills are required, however. This is the writer's favorite hike in the Monument/Palmer Lake area.

Follow the Reservoir/Ice Cave Creek route to the T intersection at 1.4 miles. Continue another 0.1 mile west to a meadow. Before crossing Ice Cave Creek again and going uphill, leave the trail and cross the meadow to a faint trail heading west-northwest that parallels Ice Cave Creek, going up and down the slope but averaging about 50 feet above the creek. Take in the view of Cap Rock—at this point, the east and south walls will make it look like an unclimbable pillar. Just beyond the third little gully coming in from the right, angle up toward the southeast corner of the base of Cap Rock. Angle in to the rocks, toward a big tree, then angle right to stay under three house-sized rocks. Work through the rocks, staying 50–75 feet to the right of the east face of Cap Rock. When the terrain begins to flatten out, look left for a scramble up to the ramp that leads to the top. Enjoy the views and the big drops down the south and east faces. Return via the same route.

PALMER LAKE RESERVOIRS AND CAP ROCK

46. Pancake Rocks and Horsethief Park

BY BILL BROWN

MAPS	Trails Illustrated, Pikes Peak/Cañon City, Number 137
ELEVATION GAIN	1,400 feet
RATING	Moderate
ROUND-TRIP DISTANCE	6.25 miles
ROUND-TRIP TIME	4 hours
NEAREST LANDMARK	Divide

COMMENT: Horsethief Park and Pancake Rocks are popular four-season destinations. Families with children and others looking for a short hike will enjoy the 3.0 mile round trip to Horsethief Falls. It's a cool escape from summertime heat in the city. The longer trail to Pancake Rocks rewards hikers with unnatural-looking stacks of saucer-shaped granite. It's hard to resist getting up close and personal to touch and climb onto some of these bizarre "pancakes."

In fall hunting season, hunters in blaze orange may be seen in Horsethief Park, reminding hikers to make themselves visible. By winter, snowshoers and backcountry skiers enjoy the area's high elevation, ample snowfall, and shaded north-facing slopes. Snow cover is usually reliable on forested slopes from late December to early April.

This entire hike is within the subalpine life zone. Blue spruce, limber pine, and aspen predominate, with some bristlecone pine at the higher elevations. The Ring the Peak Trail system, which is 80 percent complete, coincides with the Pancake Rocks Trail for about 2 miles.

GETTING THERE: From Colorado Springs, drive west on U.S. 24. Follow this highway 25 miles through Woodland Park to Divide. At the traffic light in Divide, turn left (south) on Colorado 67. At 9.1 miles, on the far side of a road cut that bypasses an abandoned railroad tunnel, there is a paved parking lot on the left with room for 10–15 cars. This is the trailhead.

THE ROUTE: The trail begins on the east side of the parking lot, just south of an interpretive sign about the history of the tunnel. After 100 yards, the trail makes a switchback to the left, and, in another 150 yards, it turns right. From here, it's a steady climb eastward on an old wagon road. After 0.5 mile on this

A great spot for a pancake breakfast.

PHOTO BY BILL BROWN

road, the trail levels out, just past a short rocky section. Hundred-year-old barbed wire fences can be seen on each side of the trail at this point, a hint of the shady history of Horsethief Park, which you are now entering. After another 0.1 mile, you intersect the Ring the Peak (RTP) Trail. To the left would take you clockwise on the ring through Putney Gulch to the Crags area. Straight ahead (east) is the way to Pancake Rocks. Another 0.25 mile ahead is a sign marking another junction. Horsethief Falls is a worthwhile destination, 0.4 mile ahead.

A right turn at the sign leads to Pancake Rocks. The next mile gains 800 feet of elevation, made easier by a series of well-constructed switchbacks. When the trail tops out, there's a view of a craggy highpoint just off the trail to the west, and distant views to the southwest. Continue on the trail, contouring generally southward, with a few minor ups and downs, for almost another mile. Cross a minor saddle; Pancake Rocks is another 600 yards to the south, through a grove of young aspen. Just before arriving, the Ring the Peak Trail diverges to the left, where it dead-ends, temporarily, pending access approvals and trail construction between here and the south slope of Pikes Peak.

At Pancake Rocks, the view opens up toward Cripple Creek and the Sangre de Cristo Mountains to the southwest. Spectacular alpine expanses of the Pikes Peak Massif draw your eyes to the east. At your feet are slabs of Pikes Peak granite, with smaller piles of rock eroded into the pancake shapes that give this special place its name.

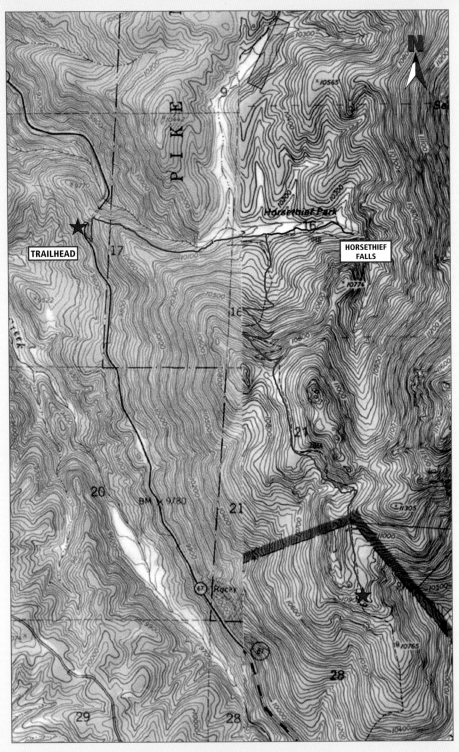

PANCAKE ROCKS AND HORSETHIEF PARK

47. Pikes Peak from the Crags

BY MATT PIERCE

MAPS	Trails Illustrated, Pikes Peak/Cañon City, Number 137
ELEVATION GAIN	4,150 feet
RATING	Difficult
ROUND-TRIP DISTANCE	12.1 miles
ROUND-TRIP TIME	7–10 hours
NEAREST LANDMARK	Mueller State Park

COMMENT: Internationally known Pikes Peak, at 14,115 feet, towers over Colorado Springs and the Front Range. Hiking Pikes Peak is a challenging endeavor. While a 12.1-mile round-trip in length, the Crags Trailhead route is a preferable hike for many to the popular Barr Trail route, which is over 25 miles long and includes 7,000+ feet of elevation gain. The weather on Pikes Peak can be unpredictable at all times of the year. Be prepared and get an early start for this full-day outing, especially in summer.

GETTING THERE: From Colorado Springs, take U.S. 24 west. At the town of Divide, turn south (left) on Colorado 67 and drive 4.3 miles. Pass the entrance for Mueller State Park, on the right, and watch for Forest Service Road 383, on the left. Turn onto this dirt road and proceed 1.6 miles to the Rocky Mountain Mennonite Camp. Turn right and continue to the entrance to the campground, at mile 3.2. Drive through the campground to the loop at the end of the road.

In the future, the Forest Service plans to move the trailhead 0.25 mile down FS Road 383 from the Crags Campground, where there will be parking for 77 cars and a new restroom. The new trail will route you north of the campground and add approximately 1.2 miles round-trip to your hike. (See proposed trail in blue on map on page 185.)

THE ROUTE: Start hiking along the Crags Trail near the parking loop. Hike a few hundred yards before reaching a trail junction. Staying left will take you on Trail #664 toward the Crags. Stay right and cross over Fourmile Creek at a small footbridge. Start gaining some elevation through the trees. Pass a sign indicating you are headed toward the Devils Playground. At 1.7 miles, near 11,250 feet, the trail turns to the right. The next 1.0 mile after making this turn is some of the steepest and most difficult of this route, gaining 1,500 feet of elevation en route to the Devils Playground, at 12,750 feet. Hike

The trail above the road.

steadily up, leaving treeline, and reach the top of the slopes at 2.75 miles near 12,750 feet. From here, the hiking is easy for the next 0.75 mile as you hike through the Devils Playground. While passing, note a small summit just to the north. This is "The Devils Playground Peak" and is Teller County's highpoint, at 13,070 feet. Visit this summit for some easy extra credit along your route.

Cross the Pikes Peak Highway at 3.5 miles (now near 13,000 feet), where the trail continues along the east side of the road. Continue hiking on the obvious trail, losing a little elevation as you parallel the road down to where it makes a right-hand curve. Tempting as it may be, hiking is NOT permitted on the Pikes Peak Highway. With the exception of crossing the road near the Devils Playground, never hike directly on the road.

Near 4.25 miles, the trail can be difficult to follow, but the route in front of you is obvious. Leave the proximity of the road and begin hiking in a more direct line toward the southeast. Pass just to the left (east) of Point 13,363, before reaching the road again, near mile 5 and 13,200 feet. Pikes Peak is to the southeast, now just 1.1 miles and 900 feet of elevation away. Hike close to the road again for 0.2 mile before the road will make a turn off to the right (southwest). Continue away from the road on the obvious path to the base of the peak. The trail can be hard to follow in the last few hundred feet to the summit, but it is marked with cairns that make navigation easier. Top out at the end of a large parking area. Hike through the parking lot to the summit house and the large sign marking the summit.

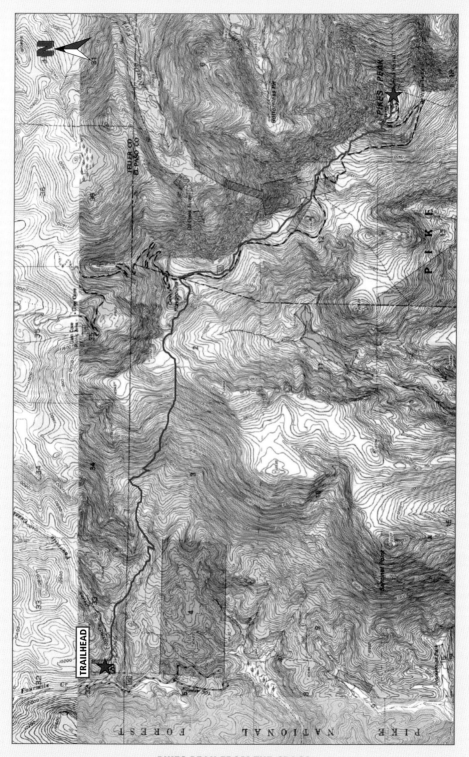

PIKES PEAK FROM THE CRAGS

48. Seven Bridges Trail to Jones Park to Mt. Buckhorn Trail Loop

BY ERIN SHAW

MAPS	Trails Illustrated, Pikes Peak/Cañon City, Number 137
ELEVATION GAIN	Loop: 2,000 feet; Seven Bridges: 1,000 feet
RATING	Loop: moderate–difficult; Seven Bridges: easy–moderate
ROUND-TRIP DISTANCE	Loop: approx. 9.5 miles; Seven Bridges: approx. 3.5 miles
ROUND-TRIP TIME	Loop: 4–5 hours; Seven Bridges: 1.5 hours
NEAREST LANDMARK	Helen Hunt Falls

COMMENT: North Cheyenne Canyon is an understandably popular destination. The Pikes Peak granite creates a stunning, craggy invitation to delve deep into the canyon. Seven Bridges is a very popular trail in the park, and offers an ideal family outing, crossing North Cheyenne Creek seven times over rustic wooden footbridges. Wildflowers are plentiful and there are many nice lunch spots along the trail. Turn after the seventh bridge, or continue to Jones Park, a valley with aspen and coniferous trees, where the trail meets Bear Creek and offers views of nearby peaks, hidden waterfalls, wildflowers, and a variety of birds.

Bicycles are allowed along the entire loop, and motorized bikes may travel the trails around Jones Park and Mt. Buckhorn. It can be more peaceful to take the hike on a weekday.

GETTING THERE: From Interstate 25, take the Nevada Avenue/Tejon Street exit 140 and proceed south 0.4 mile on South Tejon Street to the junction of Tejon, Ramona, and West Cheyenne Boulevard. Veer right (southwest) onto West Cheyenne Boulevard and drive 2.5 miles to the junction with North Cheyenne Canyon Road. The Starsmore Discovery Visitor Center is located at this junction. Turn right, entering North Cheyenne Canyon Park, and continue up North Cheyenne Canyon Road, past Helen Hunt Falls, for 3.2 miles to "the hub" parking area at the junction of Gold Camp Road, High Drive, and North Cheyenne Canyon Road.

THE ROUTE: Begin at the gate on the west end of the lot and follow a dirt road for 0.75 mile. Pass one trail to your right and look for a second trail,

Bridge Three.

just beyond a sign that reads North Cheyenne Creek. Turn right onto the trail and soon cross the first footbridge. Other trails intersect the main trail above here; stay on the trail that climbs up the canyon parallel with the creek. Over the next 1.0 mile, you will cross six more bridges. In the winter, this portion of the trail is usually covered in ice and extra traction on hiking boots is recommended.

Continue to climb through the canyon to reach Jones Park. Look for the trail just beyond the last bridge that climbs up and to the right of the creek. Views of the creek below reveal a few small waterfalls.

Signage is sparse. Social trails diverge from the main trail, but they meet it again. After rising above the creek for 0.5 mile, the trail meets the creek again. The Pipeline Trail comes in from the left (southwest) shortly after this junction; be sure to stay on the Seven Bridges Trail, heading west-northwest.

As the trail enters a mixed forest, turn left at an unmarked intersection. The trail soon meets up with the Pipeline Trail again; stay straight and don't cross the creek. Over the next 1.0 mile, stay straight on the main trail and cross two streams before coming to another unmarked intersection. Turn right and head east-southeast. Stay on the main trail as it turns right and crosses another stream. After 0.2 mile, there is a large open area where trails merge. To complete the loop, turn left onto the marked Bear Creek Trail.

Falls above Seventh Bridge.

Follow Bear Creek for about 1.3 miles to a trail junction; leave Bear Creek Trail and cross the creek to the right. Immediately begin climbing a steep ridge. After about 0.4 mile, the trail follows another ridge, rising to the right. The ridgetop affords spectacular views of Colorado Springs and Cheyenne Mountain.

For the next 1.0 mile, the trail continues to follow the north side of this ridge before meeting another ridge, which the trail now follows from the south. Shortly after leaving this ridge, an unmarked trail comes in from the right. This is the Buckhorn Cutoff Trail; follow it for approximately 1.2 miles, avoiding social trails, to rejoin the Seven Bridges Trail above the first bridge. Turn left to return to the dirt road and parking lot.

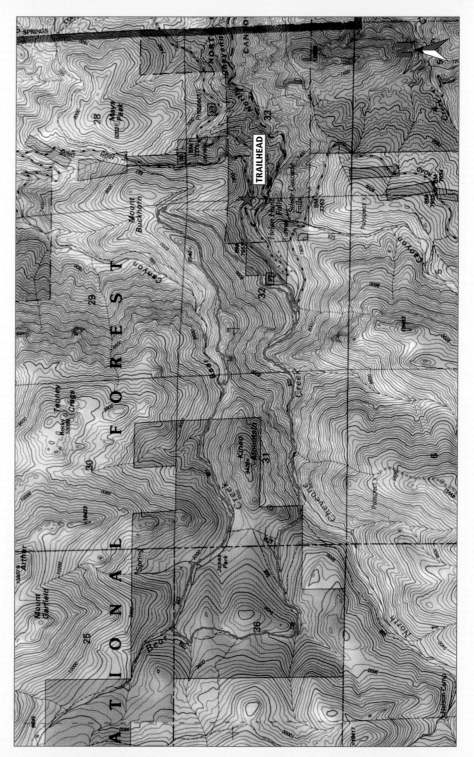

SEVEN BRIDGES TRAIL TO JONES PARK TO MOUNT BUCKHORN TRAIL LOOP

49. St. Mary's Falls Trail and Mount Rosa

BY DAN ANDERSON

MAPS	Trails Illustrated, Pikes Peak/Cañon City, Number 137 (Cuts off Mount Rosa) USGS, Manitou Springs, 7.5 minute Pikes Peak Atlas
ELEVATION GAIN	St. Mary's Falls base: 1,500 feet Mount Rosa: 4,100 feet
RATING	St. Mary's Falls base: easy–moderate Mount Rosa: moderate–difficult
ROUND-TRIP DISTANCE	St. Mary's Falls base: 6 miles Mount Rosa: 13.8 miles
ROUND-TRIP TIME	St. Mary's Falls base: 2.5–4 hours Mount Rosa: 7–10 hours
NEAREST LANDMARK	Colorado Springs, North Cheyenne Cañon Park

COMMENT: This is a great hike up a lovely side canyon of North Cheyenne Canyon. An inviting place on a hot day, the trail follows along a stream to a waterfall. It is enjoyed best in late spring and early summer when more water comes tumbling down. It can be either a hike or a snowshoe outing after a good snowfall, but be careful of ice near the falls.

GETTING THERE: From Interstate 25, take the Nevada Avenue/Tejon Street exit 140 and proceed south 0.4 mile on South Tejon Street to the junction of Tejon, Ramona, and West Cheyenne Boulevard. Veer right (southwest) onto West Cheyenne Boulevard and drive 2.5 miles to the junction with North Cheyenne Canyon Road. The Starsmore Discovery Visitor Center is located at this junction. Turn right, entering North Cheyenne Canyon Park, and continue up North Cheyenne Canyon Road, past Helen Hunt Falls, for 3.2 miles to "the hub" parking area at the junction of Gold Camp Road, High Drive, and North Cheyenne Canyon Road.

THE ROUTES:

ST. MARY'S FALLS TRAIL NUMBER 624: This hike starts at a parking area known as "the hub." It follows Gold Camp Road, which leaves past the gate at the west end of the parking lot and is currently closed to cars. The road makes

Topping out Mount Rosa.

a long horseshoe and reaches collapsed tunnel number 3. Take the trail to the left of the tunnel up and over to a trail junction. The St. Mary's Falls Trail is the right fork. The left fork goes down to Gold Camp Road, on the other side of the tunnel.

The St. Mary's Falls Trail heads south up Buffalo Canyon. The trail gains elevation slowly at first, then becomes steeper near the falls. There are a couple of switchbacks to get to the base of the falls. The trail to the falls is a 1.0 mile side trip from the second leg of the switchbacks. If you wish to continue on, eight more switchbacks will take you up the hillside. The last switchback is a long leg back to the vicinity of the creek. There is a primitive trail down to the top of the falls from here. Be careful if you go down there—the steep hillside is very treacherous near the falls.

MOUNT ROSA, NELSONS TRAIL NUMBER 672: From the top of St. Mary's Falls, the trail continues up the canyon until it reaches an old road. At this point, the standard route continues up the old road to the junction of Forest Service Road 381. This is the official end of the St. Mary's Falls Trail. Turn right (north) and go about 220 feet to the junction of Nelsons Trail on the left (west) side of the road. This trail climbs steadily, with many switch-backs, to a large shoulder on the north side of Mount Rosa. Head south along the flat to a trail junction (Trail #673) just before the terrain turns uphill. The trail curving to the right (west) goes down to Frostys Park. Continue on the trail straight ahead, which is easy to miss, as it climbs the north ridge to the top of Mount Rosa.

Pikes Peak from Mount Rosa.

On your way up Mount Rosa, there's a second, smaller shoulder. This is a great place for pictures of Pikes Peak and Almagre Mountain before reaching the summit.

After hiking up the last 500 feet, you will be treated to a grand view. Zebulon Pike called the tall peak in the distance Grand Peak; we now call it Pikes Peak. Research by John Murphy has determined that Pike probably reached Mount Rosa and turned back, declaring that Grand Peak would never be climbed.

SIDEBAR: A SIDE TRIP

Above St. Mary's Falls, where the single-track trail turns into the old road, a primitive trail branches to the left and continues up the canyon, closer to the stream. For those with good route-finding skills, this side trip is my favorite way up the canyon. If you stay with this trail, it ends 1.2 miles later at an old quarry where it meets Forest Service Road 381. Turn right and go north for 0.55 mile to the junction of the Nelsons Trail.

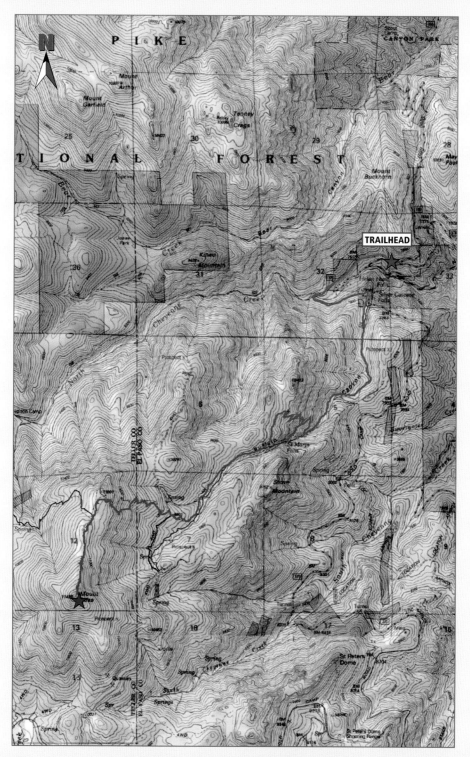

ST. MARY'S FALLS TRAIL AND MOUNT ROSA

50. Stanley Canyon Trail

BY UWE K. SARTORI

MAPS	Trails Illustrated, Pikes Peak/Cañon City, Number 137 USGS, Cascade, 7.5 minute
ELEVATION GAIN	1,450 feet
RATING	Moderate
ROUND-TRIP DISTANCE	3.8 miles
ROUND-TRIP TIME	2–3 hours
NEAREST LANDMARK	Air Force Academy Hospital

COMMENT: The U.S. Air Force Academy is a major landmark in the Colorado Springs area. Located on 18,000 pristine acres, the academy is home to the popular Stanley Canyon Trail and offers a wonderful three-season sample of the Pikes Peak area's eastern slope.

Enjoy a gentle hike beside a stream under an aspen canopy that leads into a meadow carpeted with alpine flowers, as well as steep hiking that gets the heart pumping. Challenge yourself by scrambling up granite rock. Soak in gorgeous vistas of the academy, the Black Forest area, and northern Colorado Springs—including towering granite outcroppings, alpine forests, and waterfalls. Count on varied flora and local wildlife to add color and excitement to your hiking experience.

The reward for your effort is the beautiful Stanley Reservoir. Here, you can relax and enjoy your time on the shoreline (no swimming allowed) before heading back down. Make this a day outing with a family picnic at the reservoir. Afterward, enjoy a tour of the academy grounds.

For the best experience, hike this trail between late May and early October. Late fall, winter, and early spring seasons bring winter conditions that make this trail potentially dangerous. This hike is not suitable for strollers or walkers. Mountain bikes are not recommended. The trail contains some steep, strenuous sections and requires a little scrambling.

GETTING THERE: From Interstate 25, take exit 156B–N. Entrance/Air Force Academy. Be prepared to stop at the gate and show your ID. Drive 0.5 mile and go left onto Stadium Blvd. Go 1.2 miles and turn right, onto Academy Drive. Drive 2.4 miles and turn left, onto Pine Drive. Go 0.2 mile and turn right, onto an unmarked dirt road (just past the AFA hospital). Drive 0.6 mile to the trailhead. From the south entrance of the academy, drive north

Stanley Reservoir.

on South Gate Boulevard to Pine Drive. Turn left onto Pine Drive and travel 3.9 miles to the unmarked dirt road on the left. From this direction, you will almost certainly drive past the road; turn around when you get to the hospital.

THE ROUTE: Walk past the gate at the trailhead to the road. Shortly after starting up the road, take a left fork. Less than 75 yards after the fork, a sign directs you to the right. Walk another 100 yards and turn left at the next sign for Stanley Reservoir 707.

Be ready for a mile of steep, loose dirt and gravel on the trail. While ascending, first listen, and then look, for a small waterfall to the left. Farther up, the trail will appear to overlap with a stream. Continue on, staying close and to the right of the stream. Resist the temptation to angle steeply up to the right as it leads off-trail. There are some sections that give the opportunity to do a little scrambling on the granite rock. One short section involves hopping over rocks in the stream itself. Be careful: wet rock and wet boots make for a slippery climb.

After the first mile, the trail mellows into a gentle hike. Pass through a small meadow and into a tree-canopied section over a stream crossing, complete with a makeshift log bridge. Soon, cross the stream again. For the last 0.5 mile, enjoy the trail as it alternates between meadows and trees, finally winding its way through a large meadow to the bottom of the reservoir dam. From here, a short trail to the left brings you to the shore of the reservoir.

SIDEBAR: AIR FORCE ACADEMY

The Air Force Academy visitor hours are from 8:00 a.m. to 6:00 p.m. Some of the trail is on Air Force Academy property, which means you are subject to their jurisdiction. The remainder of the trail and the reservoir is in the Pike National Forest.

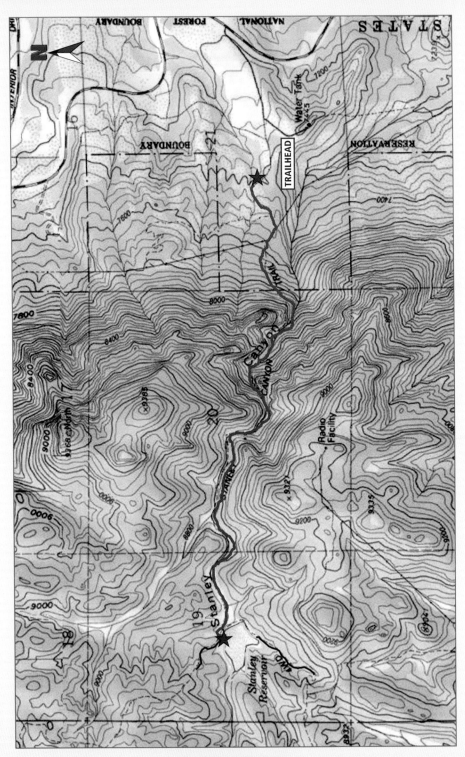

STANLEY CANYON TRAIL

51. The Crags Trail

BY ERIC SWAB

MAPS	Trails Illustrated, Pikes Peak/Cañon City, Number 137 USGS, Woodland Park/Pikes Peak, 7.5 minute
ELEVATION GAIN	724 feet
RATING	Easy–moderate
ROUND-TRIP DISTANCE	4.3 miles (5.5 miles from proposed trailhead)
ROUND-TRIP TIME	3 hours
NEAREST LANDMARK	Mueller State Park

COMMENT: The Crags Trail is a prime example of a simple hike with a great reward. After hiking through the Four Mile Creek valley with its lush meadows, rocky spires, and aspen and pine forests, you end up atop a rocky outcrop with gnarled old limber pines and great views. The Crags is a four-season favorite with hikers, skiers, and snowshoers. It receives and holds snow longer than most other areas on Pikes Peak.

GETTING THERE: From Colorado Springs, take U.S. 24 west. At the town of Divide, turn south (left) on Colorado 67 and drive 4.3 miles. After you pass the entrance for Mueller State Park on your right, watch for Forest Service Road 383 on your left. Turn onto this dirt road and proceed 1.6 miles to the Rocky Mountain Mennonite Camp. Turn right and continue to the entrance to the campground, at 3.2 miles. Drive through the campground to the loop at the end of the road. The trailhead and a restroom are at the far end of the Crags Campground Road. There is no fee for parking at the trailhead.

In winter, the road is generally plowed to the parking area just past the Mennonite Camp, so you may have to ski or snowshoe farther than indicated on the map.

In the future, the Forest Service plans to move the trailhead 0.25 mile down FS Road 383 from the Crags Campground, with a new restroom and parking for up to 77 cars. The new trail would pass north of the campground and add aproximately 1.2 miles round-trip to your hike. (See the proposed trail in blue on the map.)

THE ROUTE: A well-marked and well-traveled trail starts at the east end of the parking loop. At 0.2 mile, come to the junction of Forest Trails #664 and #753 (old #664A). Stay left on 664. (Trail #753 goes to the summit of Pikes Peak, a hike that is described on page 169.)

Along the Crags Trail.

At 1.0 mile, come to a sometimes-marshy area at the mouth of a side canyon. Cross the drainage and stay to the right of the magnificent pile of rocks ahead of you. The valley begins to narrow at 1.5 miles. On your right you will see a shallow cave near the bottom of another pile of rock. A little farther on, another trail splits off to the left; stay straight here. At 1.7 miles, begin the final climb of 300 feet to the highpoint of the Crags. Watch your footing—the decomposed granite can be very slippery.

We recommend that you return by the same route. However, if you are a good route finder you may pick up another faint trail by turning left at the rock with the cave. This is sometimes called the "Shady Side Trail" and is popular with skiers and snowshoers because it holds the snow longer. This route parallels Trail #664, but stays on the opposite side of the valley and joins Trail #753 at a sign that says Devils Playground Left, and Crags C.G., to the Right. Go to the right and you will cross the creek and arrive at the intersection of Trails #664 and #753.

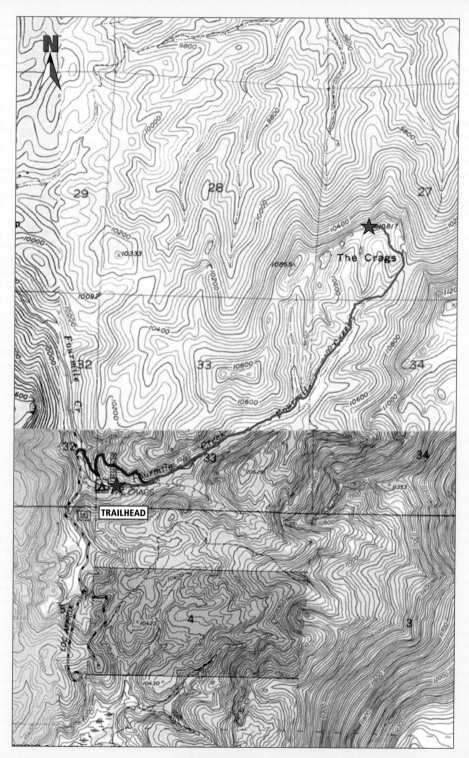

THE CRAGS TRAIL

52. American Lakes (or Michigan Lakes)

BY DON CARPENTER

MAPS	Trails Illustrated, Poudre River/Cameron Pass, Number 112
	Trails Illustrated, Rocky Mountain National Park,
	Number 200
ELEVATION GAIN	1,400 feet to the lower lake
RATING	Difficult
ROUND-TRIP DISTANCE	7.3 miles
ROUND-TRIP TIME	4–5 hours
NEAREST LANDMARK	Cameron Pass

COMMENT: This trail provides easy access to a high, wide alpine meadow experience. It travels through Colorado State Park State Forest, on the western side of the Continental Divide. The trail begins on an old logging road and climbs through evergreens and past small, snow-fed, swollen streams. To the north are views of the Diamond Peaks in the Medicine Bow Range, which extends into Wyoming. The Never Summer Range is seen to the east and south. The American Lakes, sometimes called Michigan Lakes on older maps, comprise two easily accessible lakes. A third lake, Snow Lake, involves a rocky scramble.

Depending on spring temperatures, the trail may not be easily navigable until late June or July. The Nokhu Crags (from the Arapahoe *hoh'onookee*, meaning "Eagle Rocks") form the western boundary above the lakes and shade the lakes from the late afternoon sun. As you enjoy the panoramic views of peaks and tundra, look for wildflowers like the glacier lily in late June. Other Never Summer Range views on this hike include Static Peak, with Mount Richthofen in the background, and Lulu Mountain and Thunder Mountain, all part of the Continental Divide bordering on Rocky Mountain National Park.

GETTING THERE: Take U.S. 287 north from Fort Collins to the junction of Colorado 14 at Ted's Place. Turn left (west) and proceed 62.7 miles up the Poudre Canyon to the turnoff for the trailhead. The turnoff is 2.6 miles west of Cameron Pass on the left (south) side of the road and is marked by a sign for the Crags and Lake Agnes. Continue 1.5 miles to the trailhead, following the signs for American Lakes and staying left past the Lake Agnes Trailhead.

The Nokhu Crags, a highlight of the American Lakes hike.

A parking area is at the end of the road. A state park fee or sticker is required. Alternatively, you can park at Cameron Pass, cross Colorado 14 to the south side, and follow the Michigan Ditch service road until the trail crosses the ditch and leads to the American Lakes. (Michigan Ditch collects water on the western side of the Continental Divide and diverts it to the eastern plains.)

THE ROUTE: Starting at the east end of the parking lot, follow the old logging road along the Michigan River for 1.42 miles, then cross the service road for the Michigan Ditch. Continue on the other side of the ditch, following the Michigan River on the east side of a valley, then cross the river on a wooden footbridge at 2.8 miles. Watch for wildlife, especially moose feasting on the river willows in the valley beyond the footbridge. The trail then goes through a series of switchbacks until it finally emerges from the trees. Enjoy alpine vistas of the Never Summer Range as you continue to the rock crossing at the east outlet of the lakes. (An older trail parallels the Michigan River to the lakes but is not the preferred route.) Go along the lower lake on either the north or south side to the second lake.

Time and weather permitting, you may also wish to make side trips to Thunder Pass (0.8 mile from the rock crossing and a 106-foot elevation gain), easily visible to the east along the marked trail, or on to Snow Lake. The scramble to Snow Lake is 0.5 mile farther from the rock crossing.

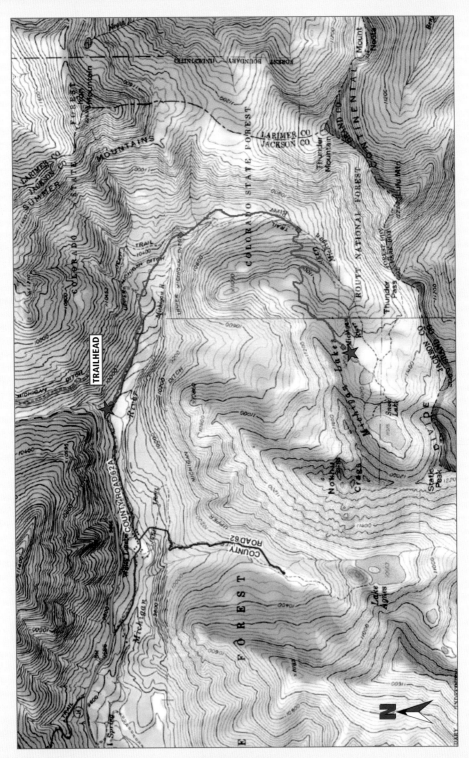

AMERICAN LAKES

53. Big South

TEXT BY EILEEN EDELMAN
PHOTO BY PAMELA CRAIG

MAPS	Trails Illustrated, Poudre River/Cameron Pass, Number 112
ELEVATION GAIN	800 feet
RATING	Easy–moderate
ROUND-TRIP DISTANCE	6 miles, up to 14 possible
ROUND-TRIP TIME	4 hours
NEAREST LANDMARK	Mile marker 75, Colorado 14

COMMENT: This hike follows the Cache La Poudre River upstream from Poudre Canyon south to Grass Creek, at mile 3, and then on to a washed-out bridge at about mile 7. Parts of the trail are lovely flat strolls on pine needles at river level; other sections climb high on the wall of the magnificent gorge formed by the river. Some spectacular sections of the trail cross large talus slopes below the gorge walls. You will enjoy the big, open rock traverses, river views, wildflowers, and luxurious forest scenery.

GETTING THERE: From Fort Collins, take U.S. 287 to Colorado 14 at Ted's Place. Turn left (west) and drive 48.7 miles, just past mile marker 75. The trailhead parking lot is on the left, just before the highway crosses a bridge. Restroom facilities are available at the campground, just beyond the bridge.

THE ROUTE: The beginning of the trail is lined with green gentian, also called monument plant. This rare plant appears as clumps of basal leaves with reddish stems when it is young, and as a tall, green-flowered, elaborate structure years later when it blooms. Continue through aspen and evergreen groves. Wonderful river scenery will be on your right, and lovely forest views will be to the left. In about fifteen minutes of moderate hiking, you will enter the Comanche Peak Wilderness Area. Look for the talus slopes on your left; they will increase in size and height as you continue walking.

The U.S. Forest Service has designated the Big South corridor as a Travel Zone, which means that camping is permitted only in designated sites. You will pass the first of these in another twenty minutes. Just beyond this campsite is the first of the open rock traverses. Stop here for a break, even just to take a picture. There are very few long, open views along this trail, but there are wonderful views up- and downstream from the rock-traverse sections. The trail is well built here, and the footing is excellent.

Along the Big South Fork of the Poudre River.

PHOTO BY PAMELA CRAIG

The second long, open traverse is just beyond campsite 5. This one is lined with wild roses, usually in flower by late June. The trail soon drops to the level of the river and a perfect picnic spot: a large boulder wall and a tree with gnarled roots provide a natural bench for several hikers. You will soon be hiking away from the river until the trail crosses a bridge over beautiful May Creek, about 2.3 miles from the trailhead. Continue for a half hour more to the top of another rock traverse. A large, open area is located here with views upstream and lots of large rocks for seating. This traverse then drops rather steeply to the point where Grass Creek comes in from the left. This is the turnaround point for a 6-mile hike.

The trail continues another 4 miles from the Grass Creek crossing to the washed-out bridge, again alternating easy-walking streamside sections with climbing rather steeply up and down the walls of the gorge. The scenery is beautiful throughout; the most dramatic views are in the first 3 miles.

SIDEBAR: A SNOWSHOE ROUTE, TOO

In winter, Big South is an excellent snowshoe trail. By early February, there should be more than enough snow to cover the rocks, and the snow lasts through early April. Against the snow, the aspen trunks that look so white in summer appear to be gold or pale green. The snow will also reveal abundant animal tracks in the open areas along the river.

BIG SOUTH

54. Black Powder Trail

BY JOHN GASCOYNE

MAPS	USGS, LaPorte, 7.5 minute
ELEVATION GAIN	500 feet
RATING	Easy–moderate
ROUND-TRIP DISTANCE	1.5 miles
ROUND-TRIP TIME	1.5–2 hours
NEAREST LANDMARK	Ted's Place, at the junction of U.S. 287 and Colorado 14

COMMENT: The Black Powder Trail begins in Gateway Park, located at the confluence of the Poudre River and the North Fork of the Poudre and is the site of the former Fort Collins water treatment plant that opened in 1903. During the Depression, Civilian Conservation Corps (CCC) workers built roads and trails in the park area. In 2004, the Picnic Rock Fire raged through much of the park. We can witness here how a natural area restores itself after a burning. In 2006, the Fort Collins Naturals Areas program began administering the park and renamed it Gateway Natural Area. Because of its natural beauty and closeness to the city, it is a popular destination—a nice hike that can be accomplished in a half day, including driving time.

Gateway Park is an inviting place, with large grassy areas, picnic pavilions, barbecue grills, and clean restrooms. As with other mountain areas, rattle-snakes are occasionally encountered, so exercise normal caution. The park is a fee area—four dollars for passenger cars and eight dollars for vans. Hours of use are 7 a.m. to 9 p.m. from Memorial Day to Labor Day, and from 8 a.m. to sunset the rest of the year.

The expression "all over the board" springs to mind as efforts are made to assess the difficulty of the Black Powder Trail. The consensus of a CMC focus group was: "easy" because it is a short distance, and "moderate" because of the elevation-gaining switchbacks. The city's Web site lists the trail as "moderate to difficult." So, if you've been looking for an "easy–moderate–difficult" hike, you've arrived. Lace up your tennies and start chugging along.

GETTING THERE: From downtown Fort Collins, take U.S. 287 about 10 miles to Ted's Place, which marks the junction with Colorado 14. Turn left (west) and go 5.3 miles on Colorado 14 to the park entrance on your right.

THE ROUTE: From the parking area, walk across the park in a northeasterly direction and cross the footbridge over the river. Stay on the dirt road for a

The North Fork of the Poudre River at Gateway Park.   PHOTO BY JOHN GASCOYNE

short distance to the sign indicating the trailhead on the right. The lower portion of the trail affords a good opportunity for aerobic exercise, as it is somewhat steep. It is, nonetheless, within the capability of most hikers. You will soon come to signage that offers a choice between staying on the trail, to the left, or going to the right to a scenic overlook. It is worth taking a few minutes to follow the short path to the overlook. There is mild exposure on this portion, so careful walking is advised. This detour also holds a wonderful example of CCC labor—a granite staircase artfully built into the trail.

Retrace your steps to the sign and continue walking up the hill and through the trees. The trail will begin to flatten out as you approach the terminus. In the proper season on this stretch, you will be treated to a kaleidoscope of wildflowers sprinkled among knee-high native grasses. Close to the top, you will come to an unmarked fork in the trail. Stay to the left for the more direct and easier path to the terminus of the trail. At the top, you will enjoy a panoramic view that includes Colorado 14 snaking through Poudre Canyon and, looking northeasterly, Seaman Reservoir and dam.

When you start back from the top, you can retrace your steps or, if you want a slightly more challenging route, follow the less-distinct portion of the trail that goes west for just a few paces and then curves around to the north. This will circle around to the fork in the trail and put you back on the main path for the trip down.

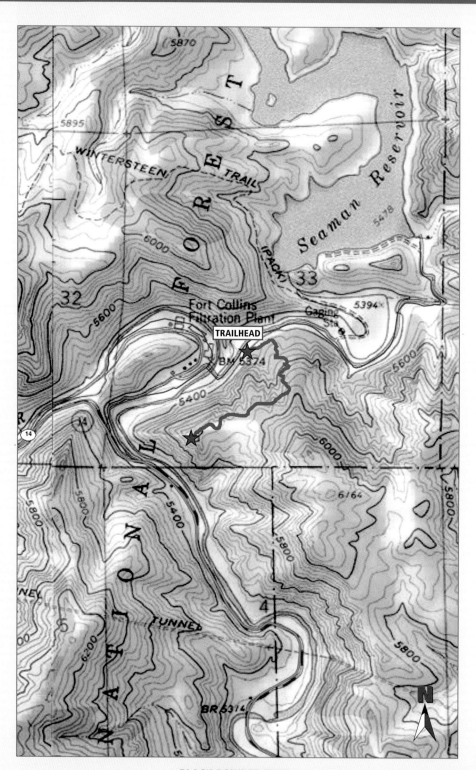

BLACK POWDER TRAIL

55. Chasm Lake

BY SANDY JORDAN

MAPS	Trails Illustrated, Rocky Mountain National Park, Number 200
ELEVATION GAIN	2,355 feet
RATING	Moderate
ROUND-TRIP DISTANCE	8.4 miles
ROUND-TRIP TIME	4–5 hours
NEAREST LANDMARK	Estes Park

COMMENT: The Chasm Lake Trail provides a classic above-treeline adventure. You will enjoy alternating views of Longs Peak, Mount Meeker, Mount Lady Washington, Twin Sisters, and Estes Cone. The trail begins below treeline as it winds through a spruce forest, then opens into an alpine meadow. Next, it traverses through an alpine wetland, complete with waterfalls, to finally summit at the tarn known as Chasm Lake. Hikers are treated to the comical antics of the marmot population, while ground squirrels, pikas, ptarmigans, and various songbirds are almost-guaranteed wildlife sightings. On occasion, you may share the trail with a pair of llamas, as the park rangers use these sturdy pack animals to restock.

GETTING THERE: From downtown Estes Park, go east on U.S. 36 and quickly turn on Colorado 7, heading south. When you come to mile marker 9, the Longs Peak Trailhead road, turn right and follow the road to the trailhead parking lot. On a given day, this lot fills up quickly and you may see cars parked along the road approaching the parking area. Park officials seem to tolerate off-road parking at this trailhead. Just beyond the ranger station, at the trailhead, is a sign-in book requesting that hikers sign in and sign back out.

THE ROUTE: The trail to Chasm Lake follows the Longs Peak Trail for the first 3.5 miles. This part of the trail follows a moderate incline over a nicely maintained footpath. About an hour out from the trailhead, a sign indicates the beginning of the tundra region. Here the trail begins to open up, and it is soon completely above treeline. Another sign, 1.7 miles from Chasm Lake, introduces a beautifully constructed stone stairway that facilitates your eleva-tion gain through the alpine tundra. The trail turns south in front of Mount Lady Washington and, about 2.5 hours from the trailhead, you will see a privy and the spur trail to Chasm Lake. Although the spur trail is only 0.7 mile long, it takes about half an hour to trek along the edge of a beautiful gorge

A golden reflection on Chasm Lake.

and through a scenic wetland. Snow on this portion of the trail often remains through the middle of July.

A second privy and a National Park Service patrol cabin mark the beginning of a fifteen-minute rock scramble up to Chasm Lake. No defined trail is present here, but multiple rock cairns indicate the general direction to the lake. Hikers who stop short of the scramble are treated to breathtaking views of the waterfalls and of the profuse wildflowers of the alpine wetland and the surrounding mountains. It is even more awe inspiring if you reach the lake. The view of the Diamond Face from the southwest corner of the lake is represented on the Colorado quarter. Consider if it is worth the extra effort to be able to hold up a quarter and tell your flatland friends that you've been there.

This hike should be undertaken only after July 1, unless you're prepared to traverse steep, narrow portions of the trail burdened with substantial snow cover. It is highly advisable to begin your hike before 8 a.m., as summer thunderstorms are quite common after the noon hour and can be particularly dangerous above treeline. A moderate pace will take you to the lake before noon. Linger at the lake just long enough for a brief rest, a short snack, and a deep inhalation of the mountain views. Pacing yourself this way, you can scurry down the trail to treeline and stay ahead of most storms.

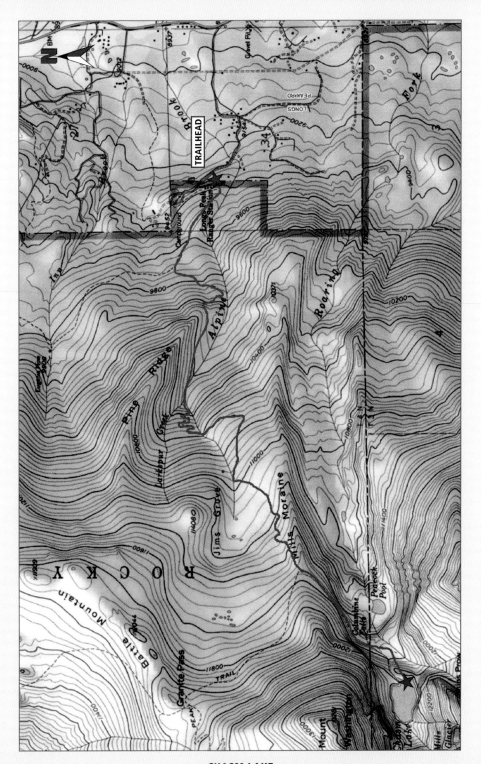

CHASM LAKE

56. Crosier Mountain

BY STEVE MARTIN

MAPS	Trails Illustrated, Cache La Poudre/Big Thompson, Number 101 USGS, Glen Haven, 7.5 minute
ELEVATION GAIN	Glen Haven Trail (931W): 2,485 feet Rainbow Trail (1013): 2,675 feet Garden Gate Trail (931E): 3,250 feet
RATING	Three trails: moderate–difficult
ROUND-TRIP DISTANCE	Glen Haven Trail (931W): 8.4 miles Rainbow Trail (1013): 7.5 miles Garden Gate Trail (931E): 9.9 miles
ROUND-TRIP TIME	Glen Haven Trail (931W): 5–8 hours Rainbow Trail (1013): 5–8 hours Garden Gate Trail (931E): 6–10 hours
NEAREST LANDMARK	Drake

COMMENT: Crosier Mountain provides a variety of hikes along three well-maintained trails that have differing elevation gains and views. The three share a steep, final, 0.5-mile spur trail to the summit, a point that offers superb vistas of Rocky Mountain National Park's high peaks. When the snow is deep, route finding can be difficult on Garden Gate Trail (931E). In August 2007, nine challenging geocaches for the keen hiker/geocacher were accessible by Crosier's trail system. Be sure to find the benchmark at the summit. Four separate "ranked peaks" form Crosier's bulk—take some time to discover them on your map and consider hiking all of them off-trail once you've whetted your appetite on the marvelous trails to the main Crosier summit.

GETTING THERE: Take U.S. 34 west from Loveland about 17 miles to Drake; turn right on County Road 43 (Devil's Gulch Road) toward Glen Haven for 2.2 miles to the Garden Gate Trailhead, on the left. Go 5.5 miles from Drake to reach the Rainbow Trailhead on the left. The Glen Haven Trailhead is at 7.3 miles, just past the horse stable at the upper end of the town of Glen Haven. All trailheads are well signed, but the trail display at Garden Gate isn't very visible from the small parking area. To access this trail, go through the small gate and up a short hill to the official information area.

THE ROUTES:

GLEN HAVEN TRAIL: Head up the dirt road as it switchbacks up the initial steep terrain; the road becomes a trail and, after about 1.5 miles, you'll arrive

Portions of the trails take you through aspen groves.

at Piper Meadows. This is a great spot for a picnic and a turnaround point for a short hike. See if you can find the foundations of Harry Piper's old farm buildings. At about an 8,000-foot elevation, ascend more switchbacks. Signage for the junction of Trails #931 and #1013 is about 2.5 miles along the trail. From here, gradually climb about 1.5 miles through lodgepole pine forests to a sign, where you'll turn right to the marvelous summit views. The final 0.5 mile is the steepest part of your hike, but the trail is enjoyable.

RAINBOW TRAIL: Hike up moderately steep terrain to a meadow at 7,600 feet and enjoy splendid views to the north and east. After 1.75 miles, you will reach Trail #931 from Glen Haven; follow it to the summit. Try to locate the old Malmberg cabin hidden below you in the trees, just southeast of the trail junction. It was built more than 100 years ago.

GARDEN GATE TRAIL: Beautiful switchbacks make the intimidating steepness of the first mile easy, and you quickly reach a large meadow that's a great location for a rest, a picnic, or a turn-back if you desire a relatively short outing. If you go farther, you will go over a saddle for a first sighting of Crosier's summit. From there, descend into True Gulch and follow the trail as it switchbacks sharply up to a sparsely treed ridge that offers spectacular views of the mountains to the south and west. After you've hiked 4.5 miles, the trail joins the Glen Haven Trail. Turn left here for the final 0.5 mile to the top.

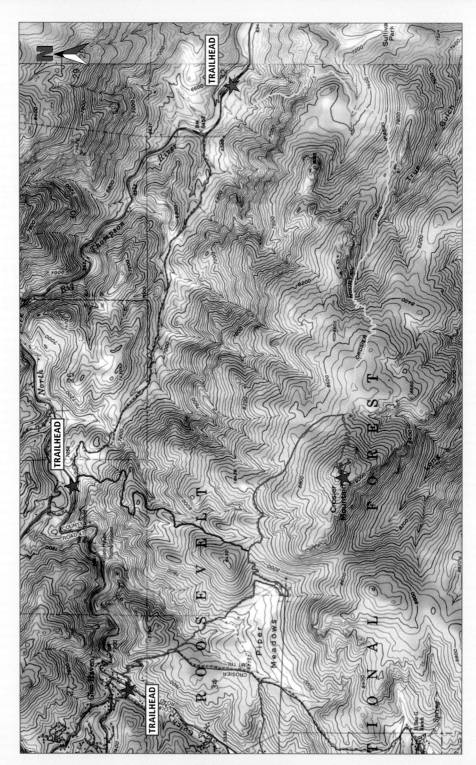

CROSIER MOUNTAIN

57. Flattop Mountain and Hallett Peak

BY TINA GABLE

MAPS	Trails Illustrated, Rocky Mountain National Park, Number 200 Trails Illustrated, Longs Peak, Number 301
ELEVATION GAIN	Flattop: 2,849 feet Hallett Peak: 3,238 feet
RATING	Difficult
ROUND-TRIP DISTANCE	10 miles
ROUND-TRIP TIME	5–6 hours
NEAREST LANDMARK	Estes Park

COMMENT: The hike up Flattop Mountain and Hallett Peak is truly a memorable experience. The switchbacks up the eastern slope of Flattop, and the last few hundred feet of rock scrambling to Hallett's summit, may be daunting for those unaccustomed to long uphill or higher-elevation hikes, but this is a well-marked trail with no technical or exposed hiking. Wildlife sightings are possible as the trail progresses up Flattop's eastern flank to the Continental Divide and one of the park's most prominently visible landmarks, Hallett Peak. Start this hike early in order to secure a parking spot at the trailhead and to avoid possible afternoon thunderstorms.

GETTING THERE: From Loveland, take U.S. 34 to Estes Park. Turn left on Moraine Avenue (U.S. 36), and continue to the Beaver Meadows Entrance Station of Rocky Mountain National Park. Go west about 0.2 mile to Bear Lake Road. Turn left and follow Bear Lake Road 9 miles to the Bear Lake parking lot.

THE ROUTE: Bear Lake and the Flattop Mountain Trailhead are located a short jaunt west from the parking lot. The summit of Hallett Peak is out of view at the beginning of your hike. Before seeing the actual summit, you will be looking at its sheer northern face and the wedge-shaped "false peak." To the north of Hallett are Tyndall Gorge and the massive hulk of Flattop Mountain. The trail to Flattop is the park's primary access to the Continental Divide, as well as the route to summit Hallett Peak.

From the eastern shore of Bear Lake, head north through the aspen grove and pine forest for 0.5 mile. Turn left at the marked Flattop/Bierstadt junction

Hallett Peak, with Flattop Mountain to the right.

and continue up the modest grade. Intermittent gaps in the trees allow views of Glacier Gorge and the imposing western flank of Longs Peak and Keyboard of the Winds.

The trail continues to wind through pine forest for another 0.5 mile to the Flattop/Fern-Odessa junction. Turn left here to continue up the Flattop Mountain Trail. Dream Lake Overlook, at 10,500 feet, offers a nice chance to rest.

Emerald Lake Overlook, at 11,300 feet, is another rest stop and provides the opportunity for some exciting photographs. Tyndall Gorge, below, and Hallett's heavily striated north face dominate this view. The summit of Hallett's Peak is clearly visible at this point, appearing as a rounded hump, approximately 400 feet higher and 0.4 mile farther west than the "false peak" that you saw from Bear Lake. The next 1.5 miles will steepen in parts, making this a more difficult section. This is a good time to drink lots of water and to take rest stops while you enjoy the striking scenery.

The last 0.25 mile starts to level out as you approach Flattop's summit. Once you are on top, the actual summit is difficult to identify, and repeat hikers no longer look for the exact highest point. You are now standing on the Continental Divide as the expanse of Bighorn Flats stretches out in front of you. To the west, you will see Grand Lake, Shadow Mountain Lake, and Lake Granby.

From the summit to the top of Hallett is another 0.5 mile and a 389-foot elevation gain. This part of the trail is considered unimproved, but the way is clearly visible to the south as you skirt the edge of Tyndall Glacier. Use caution here and do not approach the glacier's edge. The scramble up the side of Hallett is short but steep.

The top of Hallett is strewn with boulders. To the south is a five-foot-high cairn, and on the northern edge, just east of a wall of stacked boulders, is the geologic survey marker, proudly proclaiming that you are at 12,713 feet. If weather permits, enjoy a much-deserved lunch as you drink in the pano-ramic views.

Return via the same route; take your time and exercise caution when descending the rock field.

Views to the west from Continental Divide with Grand and Shadow Mountain lakes. PHOTO BY TINA GABLE

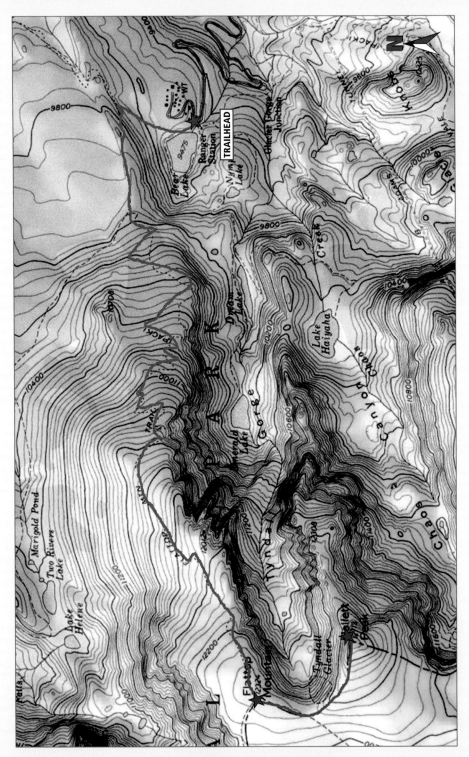

FLATTOP MOUNTAIN AND HALLETT PEAK

58. Greyrock Trail

BY ED SEELY

MAPS	Trails Illustrated, Cache La Poudre/Big Thompson, Number 101 USGS, Poudre Park, 7.5 minute
ELEVATION GAIN	2,056 feet
RATING	Moderate
ROUND-TRIP DISTANCE	6 miles
ROUND-TRIP TIME	6 hours at moderate pace
NEAREST LANDMARK	Ted's Place, at the junction of U.S. 287 and Colorado 14

COMMENT: This is a heavily used and very popular trail that is easily accessible from Fort Collins. The summit of Greyrock is of geologic interest: it is a massive granitic intrusion that has weathered to its rounded shape through exfoliation. The summit block provides popular rock-climbing routes. Watch for poison ivy along the way. The trail near the summit is not marked, and over the years hikers have become lost and required rescue help. Dogs on leash are permitted.

GETTING THERE: Take U.S. 287 north from Fort Collins about 10 miles to the Colorado 14 junction at Ted's Place. Go west on Colorado 14 about 8.6 miles to the Greyrock parking area located on the left (south) side of the highway.

THE ROUTE: From the parking lot, take the stairs down to the highway; cross carefully, as traffic can be fast moving. Take the scenic footbridge over the Poudre River to the trailhead. The trail maintains an easy grade to the lower junction with the Meadows Trail. Turn right at the lower junction to ascend the main trail along the creek. As the trail climbs the drainage, note the protective rock walls that were built during the Civilian Conservation Corps (CCC) days following the Great Depression. Respect this historic work by not walking on the walls. As you near the upper junction, a rock outcrop on the left provides a place to catch your breath and a nice overlook back down the valley. From the overlook, it is about twenty minutes farther, at a moderate pace, to the upper junction. Greyrock Peak first comes into view a short distance past this overlook. There will be a bit of elevation loss next, followed by several switchbacks leading to an open meadow and the upper junction with the Meadows Trail. This upper junction is a great spot to

Southwestern view of the far Rockies from Greyrock summit.

appreciate the bulk of Greyrock Peak. You may begin to hear voices of rock climbers at this point. After a short level stretch, the trail begins to climb along the eastern side of the peak. In places, the trail is not obvious, but rock cairns may be visible to help you stay on track. The U.S. Forest Service (USFS) has also installed several reassurance posts to help you locate the trail. Near elevation contour 7400, the trail turns back to the southwest and tops out in the summit area. You will want to note this point for your return. If the weather has not been exceptionally dry, you will see some small lakes here.

There is no marked trail from here to the peak, but, again, cairns may be visible. Cross to the southwest to begin to climb to the peak. Some scrambling and walking on sloping rock slabs is required to reach the peak, but you will be rewarded with exciting views. The plains are clearly visible to the east, with the numerous lakes of Fort Collins glinting in the sunlight earlier in the day. Snowcapped mountains are visible to the south in the Mummy Range and in the Rawahs to the west. If you start early, this is a great place to have lunch; if the weather looks threatening, have only a quick snack and begin your descent.

On your descent, take care to retrace your upward route; the descent offers the greatest likelihood of getting off-trail. Continue to watch for the small rock cairns and reassurance posts.

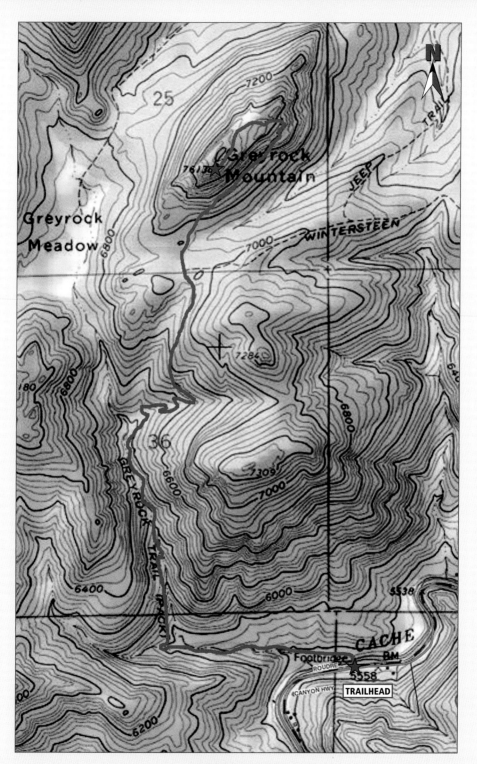

GREYROCK TRAIL

59. Hewlett Gulch

BY SANDY JORDAN

MAPS	Trails Illustrated, Cache La Poudre/Big Thompson, Number 101
ELEVATION GAIN	1,070 feet
RATING	Easy–moderate
ROUND-TRIP DISTANCE	7.8 miles
ROUND-TRIP TIME	3–4 hours
NEAREST LANDMARK	Ted's Place, at the junction of U.S. 287 and Colorado 14

COMMENT: The longest part of the popular Hewlett Gulch Trail is an easy hike, with about twenty shallow crossings through Gordon Creek. The trail follows the gulch for about 2 miles and then forms a 3.7-mile loop. In the first mile of trail, there are several stone foundations dating back to the early 1900s. Poppies and lilac bushes in this area are likely the remains of horticultural efforts by the early settlers.

Hewlett Gulch Trail offers one of the most enjoyable hikes in the lower Poudre Canyon. The profusion of wildflowers and butterflies in the spring can put a hiker on visual overload. Although the usual cautions exist for mountain lions, snakes, and bears, hikers are more likely to see fox, deer, songbirds, and lots of squirrels. The first couple of miles are easy enough for families with youngsters to enjoy. Dogs under voice control are allowed.

The trail is well populated on weekends by both two- and four-legged hikers and is also a favorite of mountain bikers. (One biker described the trail to me as "moderately technical and awesome.") Users of all kinds and species seem to respect one another, and I have never had a negative encounter on the trail.

Winter sports enthusiasts, including hard-core bikers, also find Hewlett Gulch Trail delightful. Gordon Creek adds to winter's ambience with ice-glazed rocks and frozen ripples layering over the running brook.

GETTING THERE: Take U.S. 287 north from Fort Collins about 10 miles to the Colorado 14 junction at Ted's Place. Go west on Colorado 14 about 10 miles, or 0.6 mile beyond mile marker 112. This is about 1.5 miles beyond the Greyrock Trail parking area, not far beyond the community of Poudre Park. To your right, a short bridge crosses the river and a dirt road on the left goes to the parking area and trailhead. There is a well-maintained restroom at the trailhead.

Hewlett Gulch Trailhead.

THE ROUTE: About forty-five minutes from the start of the hike, a junction with a false trail rises sharply to the left. This should not be confused with the actual loop trail, and a fallen tree trunk or branches usually discourage hikers from this option.

A short distance ahead, the trail drops about 10 feet and quickly rises again. The actual junction for the loop is just beyond this depression and is clearly marked with a rock cairn. Hikers seeking a very rigorous, steep, and rocky climb can take this left turn to begin the loop. Those of fainter heart and mellower disposition should continue along the trail; you can choose that segment of the loop on the return (downhill) portion of the trip.

Once you are past the loop junction, you will experience a rather moderate climb. About an hour into your hike, the trail narrows into a steep and rocky but short climb, then opens into a vast meadow. Here the trail becomes a double track on a moderately inclined path, merging alternately to single track up to the summit.

The trail eventually appears to end at a T, but observant hikers will notice a left turn to complete the loop. Taking the trail to the right will lead to an overlook near Diamond Rock. You can look down upon the Poudre River and Colorado 14 from this overlook, but there is no access to the parking area or the highway from here. Thus, take the left turn to stay on the loop and to begin your return portion of the hike.

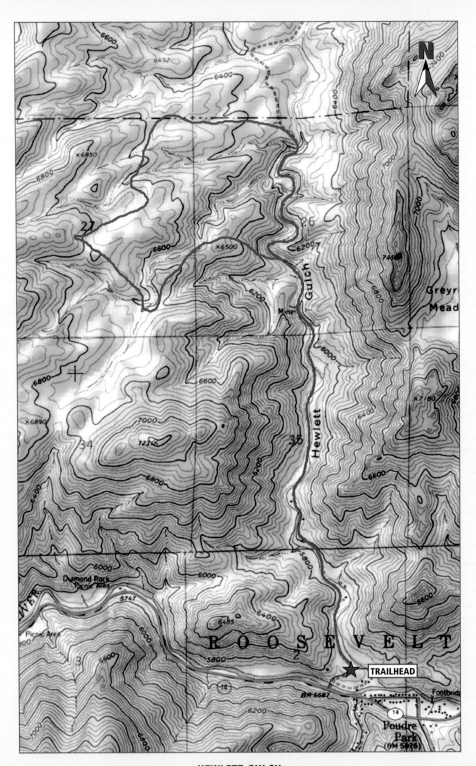

HEWLETT GULCH

60. Montgomery Pass Trail (#986)

BY JOE AND FRÉDÉRIQUE GRIM

MAPS	Trails Illustrated, Poudre River/Cameron Pass, Number 112
	USGS, Clark Peak, 7.5 minute
ELEVATION GAIN	1,049 feet
RATING	Moderate but short
ROUND-TRIP DISTANCE	3.8 miles
ROUND-TRIP TIME	3 hours
NEAREST LANDMARK	Cameron Pass

COMMENT: This is a four-season trail that quickly takes you above timberline as it climbs up to Montgomery Pass. The trail provides an enjoyable short hike in the summer, and it can serve as a good jumping-off point for longer trips to nearby peaks in the Medicine Bow Range, such as Diamond Peaks and Clark Peak. In the winter, the trail is popular with snowshoers and backcountry skiers on their way up to the bowls of Diamond Peaks. The climb up to the pass is pleasant as you pass through evergreen forest interspersed with a few small meadows. The pass itself is the prize, however, as it has magnificent views of the surrounding peaks and ranges and down into North Park. But don't just focus your sights on the mountain vistas; a host of beautiful alpine flowers grow here in the late spring and into early summer.

GETTING THERE: From Fort Collins, go north about 10 miles on U.S. 287 to Ted's Place and turn left (west) onto Colorado 14. Follow Colorado 14 up the Cache la Poudre Canyon 56.4 miles to the Zimmerman Lake Trailhead. The trail begins on the opposite side of the road, on the north side of the parking lot, and is indicated by a small sign.

THE ROUTE: The trail begins at an elevation of 9,987 feet. Start by gradually climbing to the north, generally paralleling the highway, while making your way through spruce forest. At Montgomery Creek, turn sharply left and head upstream, following an old jeep road along the creek. Here the trail starts to climb moderately toward the west. After half a mile, you leave the creek and climb more steeply for a while, along a ridge. As the trail gets higher, you will pass through a few small meadows. At the 1.4-mile mark, you will reach the remnants of an old cabin that some believe belonged to settler Tom Montgomery around 1900. Just past the cabin is a sign that says to turn right

Montgomery Pass in winter.

to go to Montgomery Pass. (Turning left and following the signage "to the bowls" would take you steeply up to timberline and to an old mine. This is the route frequently taken by backcountry skiers to reach the bowls, which lie farther to the south, below Diamond Peaks. Be aware: there can be significant avalanche danger in the bowls, and fatalities have occurred there in the past. It is critical to check avalanche conditions before you leave.) From here, the climb becomes less steep, and after 0.33-mile you will reach timberline and, shortly after, Montgomery Pass and an elevation of 10,998 feet. The views from the pass are awesome. You can see down into North Park and across to the Park Range. Looking in the other direction, you can view the Mummy Range to the southeast and the Never Summer Range to the south.

You can turn around here or continue to hike from the pass. To the south of the pass is a faint trail that leads to the old mine and to the trail that goes to the end of the bowls. You can also reach the 11,700-foot Diamond Peaks by following the ridgeline south for 1.5 miles. A faint jeep trail along the ridge leads to the identically named Montgomery Pass Trail, in Colorado State Forest State Park. Continue to follow the ridgeline 5 miles to the north to arrive at Clark Peak; at 12,951 feet, this is the sentinel of the Medicine Bow Range.

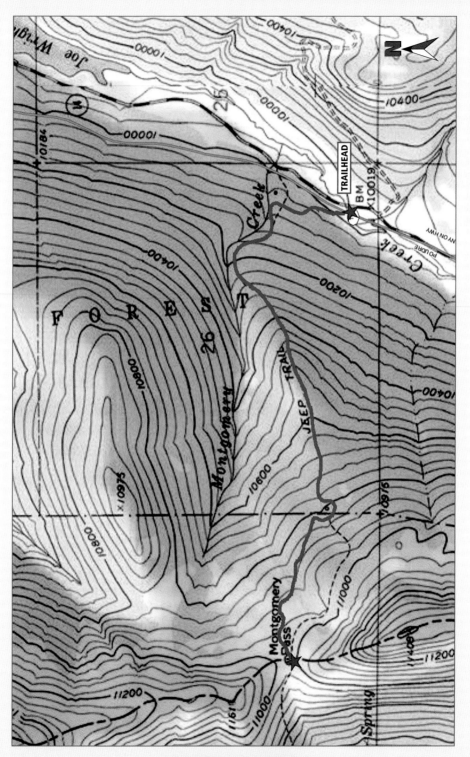

MONTGOMERY PASS TRAIL

61. Mount Margaret

BY JOHN GASCOYNE

MAPS	Trails Illustrated, Red Feather Lakes/Glendevy, Number 111
ELEVATION GAIN	Minus 137 feet
RATING	Easy
ROUND-TRIP DISTANCE	8 miles
ROUND-TRIP TIME	3–4 hours
NEAREST LANDMARK	Red Feather

COMMENT: "This is what I call solvency," my friend exclaimed as he finished a 360-degree pirouette on the top of Mount Margaret. This was the lead-in to a lunch-break discussion of how we can never go broke as long as the striking views, the chipmunks skittering across the rocks, an eagle windsurfing a thermal updraft, and restorative solitude remain available to us at such places. Forget that the crest of Mount Margaret is lower than the trailhead and that there is little perceptible elevation change between the two. When you reach the top, it feels like the top. Oh yes, ascending to the very, very top is not at all recommended: it consists of a dome about 30 feet high and, without climbing gear, could not be scaled without significant exposure.

GETTING THERE: From the intersection of Shields and U.S. 287 on the northwest side of Fort Collins, go 17 miles west and then north on U.S. 287 (going past the turnoff to Poudre Canyon) to the Livermore Junction. Turn left onto County Road 74E; go 20 more miles and watch for the trailhead parking lot on your right. Note that you will be asked to close the gate behind you; cattle graze this part of the Roosevelt National Forest.

THE ROUTE: The trail to Mount Margaret is straightforward and there is generally good signage where other trails intersect with the main trail. Early on in your hike, you will come to a medium-size stream. To avoid wading, look for a narrow path somewhat to your right once you have the stream in sight. This will take you to a narrow but stable footbridge over the stream. Bear to your left after crossing and you will be back on the trail. Another mile or so will bring you to another gate and another chance to practice bovine etiquette on the trail. Shortly after, there is a fork in the path, and you will want to stay to the right. About 2.5 miles along the trail, you will come to what some maps describe as the Five Points intersection. You have an array of trail choices here, two on your left that lead to Dowdy Lake and one

Mount Margaret Trail, close to the summit.

that is part of a loop trail off of the main trail. A soft right turn will keep you on the main trail; a nearby sign will verify that you are on the proper path. For the most part, the trail to Mount Margaret feels very open and more like you are hiking the high plains rather than a mountainous path. As you begin to move up to the summit, however, you will experience a somewhat abrupt change in the topography and feel more like you are in the high Colorado mountains. As you sit at the summit contemplating the wonderful view, consider that you are more than 100 feet lower than the trailhead where you started. This seeming incongruity only tells us that there is a gradual and barely recognizable downslope throughout much of the trail.

Shorter routes to Mount Margaret are possible by driving past the trailhead, then going through Red Feather and on to Dowdy Lake. Depending upon which of two alternative trails you take, you can shave at least a mile from the 4-mile hike to the top.

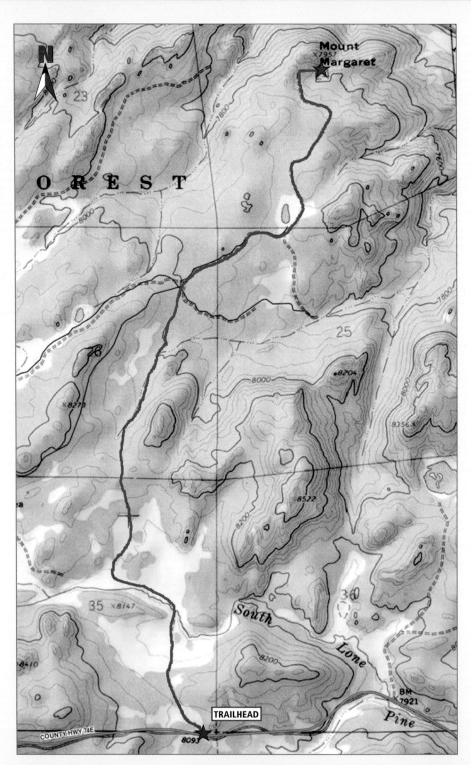

MOUNT MARGARET

62. Mount McConnell

BY LISA BARKLEY
PHOTO BY ANDREW C. GORIS

MAPS	Trails Illustrated, Cache La Poudre/Big Thompson, Number 101 (2003 version has errors) USGS, Big Narrows, Roosevelt National Forest, 7.5 minute
ELEVATION GAIN	1,327 feet
RATING	Easy–moderate
ROUND-TRIP DISTANCE	4.8 miles
ROUND-TRIP TIME	4 hours
NEAREST LANDMARK	Ted's Place, at the junction of U.S. 287 and Colorado 14

COMMENT: The McConnell Summit Trail is a short and scenic loop hike in the Cache La Poudre Wilderness, with great views of the Poudre Canyon, Poudre River, and surrounding mountain ranges.

There is a four-dollar fee for day use; drinking water and restrooms are available at the trailhead. Although the parking lot is closed in winter, the lower elevation of the area makes hiking possible during most of the year. Caution should be used in winter months, however, as much of the trail is north facing and may have snow. Dogs on a leash are allowed.

The Cache La Poudre Wilderness is a small wilderness area of 9,400 acres and is crossed by the Poudre River and the Little South Fork of the Poudre River. Mount McConnell and Bear Mountain are the only two named peaks in the wilderness area, according to the USGS map. There are only two maintained trails in the area: the McConnell Summit Trail, described here, and the Kreutzer Nature Trail. The Summit Trail loops off of the Kreutzer Trail.

GETTING THERE: From downtown Fort Collins, head north about 10 miles on U.S. 287 until you reach Ted's Place, at the junction with Colorado 14. Turn left and go west on Colorado 14 for about 23.5 miles. Turn left off of Colorado 14 and cross a bridge over the Poudre River to the Mountain Park Recreation Area sign. Make an immediate right turn to the parking lot.

THE ROUTE: Start from the trailhead at the lower parking lot and hike the loop in a counterclockwise direction. The trail ascends steeply with numerous switchbacks. Just short of the 0.5-mile point, there is an overlook of the campground. As you ascend the trail, you will view the Poudre River, the surrounding mountains, and Colorado 14 to the north. The switchbacks will continue.

The view from Mount McConnell.

At 0.8 mile, you will reach a junction for the Kreutzer Nature Trail. Turn right (west) to stay on the McConnell Trail (marked as Trail #992). For the quicker loop, keep going straight on the Kreutzer Trail (Trail #936). At a bit over a mile, you'll see a scree field. At the edge of this field is a small rock wall that can be used as a rest area or as a good site to take photos of your hiking companions.

At 1.25 miles, the trail opens up and provides wonderful views, including the Mummy Range to the west. A 300-foot side trail branches off to the west and rewards you with a bird's-eye view of the Poudre River down below.

You'll find interesting rock formations as you continue on. At nearly 2 miles, the trail branches right (west) to the McConnell summit. At slightly more than 2 miles, you reach the summit and can enjoy a panoramic over-look. This is a great place to relax; large boulders provide several places to get out of the wind, if that is a factor.

From here, backtrack to the main trail to continue. (Distances beyond this point include the round trip to the summit.) After a short way, you'll find an interesting rock bench on the left and a short spur going to another nice view.

The trip down is steeper and more rugged than the ascent. This section makes the hike a bit more challenging, but it is worth the effort. However, if you want to avoid this portion, you could make this an out-and-back hike by going to the summit and returning on the same section of trail.

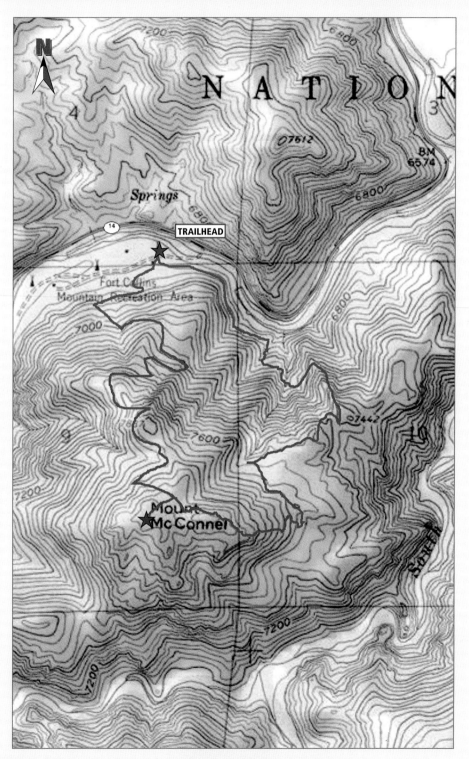

MOUNT McCONNELL

63. Stormy Peaks Trail to Stormy Peaks Pass

BY JEFF EISELE

MAPS	Trails Illustrated, Poudre River/Cameron Pass, Number 112 USGS, Pingree Park, 7.5 minute
ELEVATION GAIN	2,700 feet
RATING	Moderate
ROUND-TRIP DISTANCE	11.2 miles
ROUND-TRIP TIME	6–8 hours
NEAREST LANDMARK	Ted's Place, at the junction of U.S. 287 and Colorado 14

COMMENT: The Stormy Peaks Trail to Stormy Peaks Pass begins in Roosevelt National Forest near the entrance to Colorado State University's Pingree Park mountain campus. It travels through portions of the national forest, the Comanche Peak Wilderness, and north Rocky Mountain National Park.

Hikers who wish to continue beyond this described hike, to the Stormy Peaks summits, will scramble over grassy slopes and large boulders an additional 0.2 mile and 475 feet higher to the west summit at 12,148 feet. After that, it's another 0.5 mile with an additional 50 feet of climbing to the east summit at 11,986 feet.

This well-defined trail offers a wide variety of hiking experiences, traveling through part of the 1994 Hourglass Fire burn area, where new growth is established. It then goes through aspen, spruce, and lodgepole pine forest on to timberline and rolling tundra abundant with wildflowers.

Your hike includes expansive views of the Mummy Range and the Never Summer Range to the west and north. The drainage of the North Fork of the Poudre River is visible to the north and, in its upper reaches, panoramas of the Front Range foothills. To the south, you will have vistas of Rocky Mountain National Park (RMNP).

GETTING THERE: From downtown Fort Collins, go north on U.S. 287 about 10 miles to Ted's Place, then turn left and go west on Colorado 14 for approximately 26 miles to County Road 63E, also known as the Pingree Park Road. Turn left and go south on County Road 63E approximately 16 miles to the Stormy Peak Trailhead. (Note that after 12 miles, County Road 63E merges with County Road 44H.) The trailhead parking lot is across the road

Why we love Colorado.

PHOTO BY JEFF EISELE

from the Pingree Park campus entrance. In good conditions, your drive will take about 90 minutes.

THE ROUTE: After four switchbacks in the first 0.5 mile, the rocky trail follows a mostly south-southwest path for 2.7 miles, then goes in a south-southeasterly direction to the pass. It crosses junctions with trails to Denny's Point, at 0.6 mile from the trailhead, and Twin Lakes Reservoir, at 0.9 mile. At 2.7 miles from the beginning, you will enter the wilderness and then, after 3.5 miles, RMNP. Dogs are not allowed on the trail after this point.

Approximately 4.3 miles into the hike, rock cairns begin to mark the route and help guide you through the only area where you might stray off-trail.

The Stormy Peaks North campsite is at 4.5 miles, and just beyond, at 4.7 miles, timberline begins at an elevation of 11,000 feet. A backcountry/wilderness permit from RMNP is required for overnight stays at the campsite.

From here to the pass, you will hike through tundra with a wide variety of wildflowers in spring and summer. Columbine, bluebells, Indian paintbrush, cinquefoil, and many other flowers color the landscape.

As you continue, look to the east for a summit with a large boulder seemingly balanced on end. This is a false summit. The true west Stormy Peaks summit is farther east and comes into view as you near the pass.

At the pass, with the summits beyond, you can peer into the valley where the North Fork of the Big Thompson River runs. You can also see Comanche Peak and Fall Mountain to the northwest and, to the south and southwest, Mount Dickinson, Mount Dunraven, Mummy Mountain, Hagues Peak, Rowe Peak, and Rowe Mountain.

From the pass, follow the same route back to the trailhead.

STORMY PEAKS TRAIL TO STORMY PEAKS PASS

64. Twin Crater Lakes

BY DAVID WASSON

MAPS	Trails Illustrated, Poudre River/Cameron Pass, Number 112 USFS, Rawah Lakes, Boston Peak
ELEVATION GAIN	2,500 feet
RATING	Moderate
ROUND-TRIP DISTANCE	13 miles
ROUND-TRIP TIME	6–8 hours
NEAREST LANDMARK	Cameron Pass

COMMENT: The Twin Crater Lakes are near the middle of the Rawah Wilderness Area and provide a full-day hike through old-growth forests to a rewarding destination below steep, rocky ridges and mountain summits. Sturdy log bridges allow crossings of the West Branch of the Laramie River. In early summer, flower lovers can enjoy an array of beautiful displays from wild iris and penstemon to avalanche lilies and Jacob's ladder. Birding enthusiasts may spot a red-naped sapsucker, pygmy nuthatch, or broad-tailed hummingbird. Big-game sightings include deer, elk, moose, and bighorn sheep. In the higher elevations of the Rawahs, snow can remain into early summer, and access to the trailhead via the Laramie River Road is limited by snow closure for several months each year.

If you want to extend your hike beyond the Twin Crater Lakes, following the West Branch Trail to its terminus will lead to Carey Lake and Island Lake. These lakes offer another beautiful destination for a full-day trip in the Rawahs, with outstanding views of Cameron Peak, at 12,127 feet, and Clark Peak, at 12,951 feet.

Hot summer days can bring mosquitoes from the still water in the area, so plan ahead and pack insect repellent. These trails are horse-friendly, and you may encounter equestrians while you are hiking. Fires are prohibited above timberline in the Rawah Wilderness.

GETTING THERE: From Fort Collins, head north on U.S. 287 for about 10 miles to Ted's Place. Turn left (west) on Colorado 14 and go 52 miles to the Laramie River Road. Turn right (north) and follow the road 7 miles, passing Tunnel Campground, to the West Branch Trailhead. Toilets are available at the trailhead.

THE ROUTE: From the trailhead, the West Branch Trail heads south

A 12,240-foot ridge rises above Twin Crater Lakes and the North Fork Trail.   PHOTO BY DAVID WASSON

alongside the road and turns west for a short distance, then crosses a large bridge south to the dirt trail. Your hike continues west as a pleasant route in the Rawah Wilderness Area. As the trail continues west, it crosses several small streams in the first 2.5 miles before reaching the Camp Lake Trail. Continue southwest on the West Branch Trail along a gentler grade for another mile, where the trail will intersect with the Rawah Trail. Take the Rawah Trail west and enjoy the old-growth spruce and fir forests in this wild area.

After a mile, the trail rises more steeply and crosses two wide log bridges. Continue up the switchbacks to the intersection with the North Fork Trail. Turn left, heading southwest on this trail until you reach timberline and a splendid view of steep ridges in the Rawahs. The high falls on the ridge to the northwest drain from Rockhole Lake, at 11,200 feet. South Rawah Peak rises above, at 12,644 feet. Continue on the trail, heading southwest, and stay on the west side of the drainage. The trail turns, and you will go south until you near the first of the Twin Crater Lakes. The diamond-shaped high point on the ridge, at 11,680 feet, provides a dramatic backdrop to your adventure. To return, retrace your route back to the trailhead.

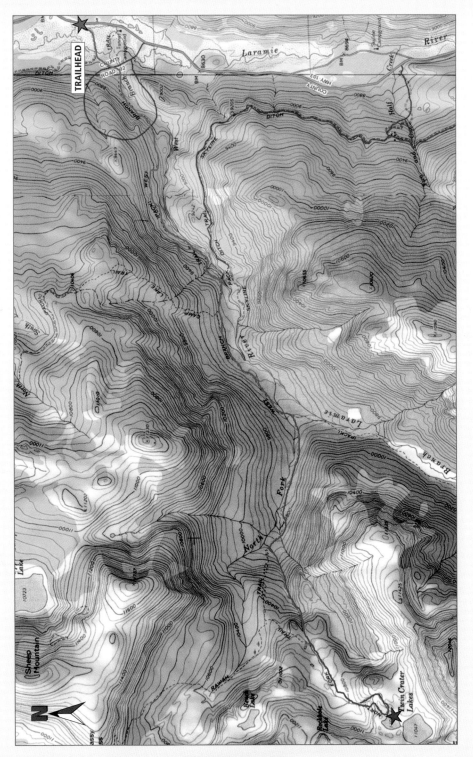

TWIN CRATER LAKES

65. Vedauwoo/Turtle Rock Loop

BY ANN HUNT

MAPS	USGS, Sherman Mountains East, 7.5 minute
	USGS, Sherman Mountains West, 7.5 minute
ELEVATION GAIN	Less than 100 feet
RATING	Easy
ROUND-TRIP DISTANCE	2.8 miles
ROUND-TRIP TIME	1.5 hours
NEAREST LANDMARK	Laramie, Wyoming

COMMENT: The Vedauwoo (VAY-duh-voo) area, "land of the earth-born spirit" in the Arapaho dialect, is a wonderful array of stunning granite formations that both intrigue the eye and beckon the body to try a bit of rock scrambling. This 7,600-acre oasis sits on the Wyoming high plains at an elevation of 8,000 feet. Ponderosa pine, Douglas fir, and aspen trees add to Vedauwoo's natural beauty. The aspen trees offer a golden delight in the early autumn. The area is home to small mammals, deer, antelope, and domestic cattle. The winds seem to always blow, sculpting the land and giving soaring rides to the native raptors that nest in many hideaways among the rock pinnacles. This is a good destination for all seasons: spring, summer, and fall hiking, rock climbing, and camping—both in established and at primitive sites. In winter, you can enjoy crosscountry skiing and snowshoeing.

The dramatic landscape invites the casual and professional photographer in every season, and extraordinary views of granite spires and domes provide unique photo opportunities. Vedauwoo is a favorite destination for rock climbers, who can be seen clinging to the rock like colorful spiders.

The Turtle Rock Loop is suitable for families with young children, and there are four restrooms near the trail.

GETTING THERE: From Fort Collins, take U.S. 287 to Laramie, Wyoming, and then take Interstate 80 17 miles southeast to exit 329, the Vedauwoo exit. Drive east on Forest Service Road 700, which is paved, to the campground entrance. There is a fee for day use if you park near the east or west Turtle Rock trailheads in the campground area. If you don't mind a little extra walking, free parking is available about 0.3 mile east on the gravel portion of Forest Service Road 700, past the campground entrance and on the north side of the road. There is also a fee for overnight camping.

Majestic views abound at Vedauwoo.

THE ROUTE: The trailhead is accessed from a paved parking area about 0.2 mile from the entrance kiosk. You can take the trail west from the lower parking area or go east from the upper parking area—the route described here. Your hike consists of an easy walk around a granite dome, aptly named Turtle Rock. At many points along the trail there are interesting rock formations to investigate and enjoy. From the east trailhead, walk through a pine and aspen woodland near the campground road, go through a gate, and continue past a stream running among large boulders. Next, pass a riparian area choked with willows. You will soon gain good views of flat meadows surrounded by the granite spires and pinnacles of the Devils Playground. As you head west, marvel at the large granite formations and the rocks balanced precariously above you. Take note of the beaver dams built in the nearby stream. Follow the path through stands of aspen and proceed through another gate. When you reach the western trailhead, you will quickly realize that you have completed the loop.

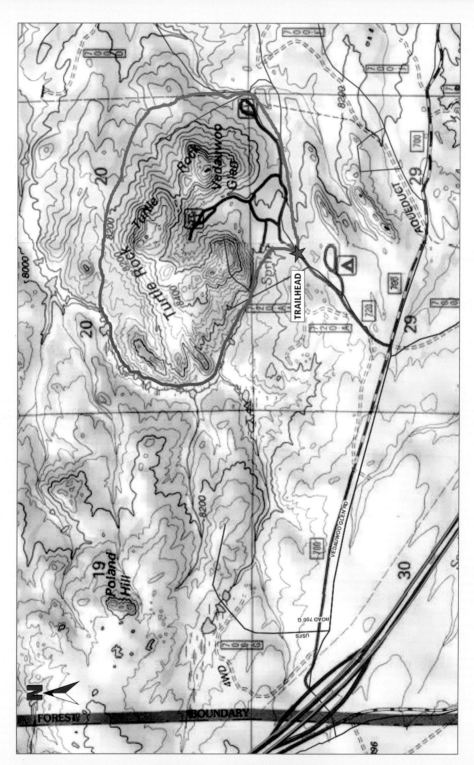

VEDAUWOO / TURTLE ROCK LOOP

Checklist of Hikes

ROUTE	PAGE	HIKING PARTNER	DATE
☐ Abyss Lake	26		
☐ American Lakes	186		
☐ Arapaho Pass and Caribou Pass	93		
☐ Barr Trail to Pikes Peak	141		
☐ Bear Peak Loop	97		
☐ Beaverbrook Trail	32		
☐ Ben Tyler Trail to Kenosha Ridge	35		
☐ Bergen Peak	38		
☐ Big South	189		
☐ Black Lake	100		
☐ Black Powder Trail	192		
☐ Blue Lake	103		
☐ Carpenter Peak	41		
☐ Catamount Trail	195		
☐ Chasm Lake	145		
☐ Chicago Lakes	44		
☐ Chief Mountain and Squaw Mountain	47		
☐ Citadel, The	50		
☐ Crags Trail, The	183		
☐ Crosier Mountain	198		
☐ Diamond Lake	106		
☐ Eldorado Canyon Trail	109		
☐ Flattop Mountain and Hallett Peak	201		
☐ Green Mountain via Gregory Canyon	113		
☐ Greyrock Trail	205		
☐ Heart Lake	116		
☐ Herman Lake	59		
☐ Hewlett Gulch	208		
☐ James Peak and St. Mary's Glacier	62		
☐ Lizard Rock—Lake Park Loop	148		
☐ Long Scraggy Peak	68		
☐ Lovell Gulch	151		
☐ Maxwell Falls	71		

ROUTE	PAGE	HIKING PARTNER	DATE
☐ McCurdy Mountain	154		
☐ Meadow Mountain and St. Vrain Mountain	119		
☐ Mesa Trail	122		
☐ Montgomery Pass Trail	211		
☐ Mount Audubon	125		
☐ Mount Bancroft and Parry Peak	29		
☐ Mount Edwards and McClellan Mountain	53		
☐ Mount Flora, Colorado Mines Peak, and Mount Eva	56		
☐ Mount Herman	157		
☐ Mount Margaret	214		
☐ Mount McConnell	217		
☐ Mount Parnassus and Woods Mountain	74		
☐ Mount Sanitas	128		
☐ Mount Sniktau and Grizzly Peak	83		
☐ Mueller State Park — Cheesman Ranch and Outlook Ridge Geer Pond Loop	160		
☐ Palmer Lake Reservoirs and Cap Rock	163		
☐ Pancake Rocks and Horsethief Park	166		
☐ Pawnee Pass	131		
☐ Pegmatite Points	77		
☐ Pikes Peak from the Crags	169		
☐ Rosalie Peak	80		
☐ Seven Bridges Trail	172		
☐ Square Top Mountain	86		
☐ St. Mary's Falls Trail and Mount Rosa	176		
☐ Stanley Canyon Trail	180		
☐ Stormy Peaks Trail to Stormy Peaks Pass	220		
☐ Torreys Peak via the Kelso Ridge	65		
☐ Tour D'Abyss, The: Mount Bierstadt and Mount Evans	89		
☐ Twin Crater Lakes	223		
☐ Twin Sisters Peaks	134		
☐ Vedauwoo/Turtle Rock Loop	226		
☐ Walker Ranch Loop	137		

The Most Popular Hiking Guides to The Front Range

The Best Denver Hikes
Denver Group, CMC, with Bob Dawson
144 pages, ISBN 978-0-9799663-5-4, $15.95

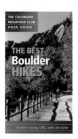

The Best Boulder Hikes
Boulder Group, CMC, with Jim Groh
104 pages, ISBN 978-0-9799663-4-7, $12.95

The Best Colorado Springs Hikes
Pikes Peak Group, CMC, with Greg Long
104 pages, ISBN 978-0-9799663-6-1, $12.95

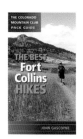

The Best Fort Collins Hikes, John Gascoyne
96 pages, ISBN 978-0-9799663-0-9, $14.95.

**Available at bookstores and outdoor stores throughout Colorado,
or order from
www.cmc.org**

Get Outside.

COLORADO MOUNTAIN CLUB

Become a CMC Member, today!

Explore the mountains and meet new people with the Colorado Mountain Club. Join us for trips, hikes, and activities throughout the state! Join today and save with special membership promotions for our readers:
www.cmc.org/readerspecials

The Colorado Mountain Club is the state's leading organization dedicated to adventure, recreation, conservation, and education. Founded in 1912, the CMC acts as a gateway to the mountains for novices and experts alike, offering an array of year-round activities, events, and schools centered on outdoor recreation.

When you join the Colorado Mountain Club, you receive a variety of member benefits including:

- 20% member discount on CMC Press books
- 15% member discount on CMC hats, t-shirts, and hoodies
- 40% off admission to the American Mountaineering Museum
- Discounts at various outdoor retailers
- 4 issues of *Trail & Timberline* magazine
- FREE signups to over 3,000 mountain adventures annually
- Access to courses, classes, and seminars throughout the state
- Adventure Travel opportunities to take you to the world's great destinations